Tools for Ministry

Equipped for the Work of Building Up the Body of Christ

Matthew Allen

Published by
Spiritbuilding Publishers
9700 Ferry Road, Waynesville, OH 45068

TOOLS FOR MINISTRY
Equipped for the Work of Building Up the Body of Christ

By Matthew Allen

ISBN 978-1-964-80557-3

Spiritbuilding
PUBLISHERS

spiritbuilding.com

Table of Contents

Preface

It has been my privilege to prepare this material for our study together. It is my prayer that each of us will come to see more clearly the vision Christ has for His church: a body where every member is equipped and every Christian is engaged in the work of ministry. The New Testament makes clear that ministry is not reserved for a few select leaders but is the shared responsibility of the entire body of Christ. By inspiration of the Spirit, the apostle Paul affirmed that Christ "gave some to be apostles, some prophets, some evangelists, some pastors and teachers, to equip the saints for the work of ministry, to build up the body of Christ" (Ephesians 4:11–12). Each member has been given a manifestation of the Spirit for the common good, and the health of the church depends on the faithful use of these gifts.

This workbook, *Tools for Ministry*, reflects a conviction that has shaped my own life and ministry: the strength of the church does not rest on the work of a few, but on the faithful service of the many. Each of us has been entrusted with gifts, opportunities, and responsibilities to use for the good of others and for the glory of God. When we embrace that calling, the body of Christ grows strong, healthy, and effective in its mission.

Throughout this study, we will explore both the foundations and the practices of ministry. We will learn how Scripture and prayer shape us, how encouragement and service sustain us, how relationships and hospitality bind us together, and how endurance equips us to persevere. Lessons are designed to move beyond theory into practice, rooted in biblical teaching and strengthened through active participation. Discussions and guided conversations will highlight diverse experiences of ministry, demonstrating how the principles of God's Word take shape in real life. You will be invited to consider your own strengths and opportunities for service and to commit yourself to specific actions that build up the body of Christ.

It is my hope that these lessons will not remain on the page but will take root in your life, producing fruit in your home, in this congregation, and in every place God sends you. By the end of this quarter, may each of us have a clearer understanding of our personal role in God's mission and a stronger resolve to carry it out. As Paul wrote, "the whole body, fitted and knit together by every supporting ligament, promotes the growth of the body for building up itself in love by the proper working of each individual part" (Ephesians 4:16).

In Christ,

Matthew Allen

October 2025

Introduction

The mission of Christ calls every disciple into active service. From the earliest days of the church, Christians were not only taught but also equipped to live out their faith in practical ways. The New Testament consistently emphasizes that ministry is shared among all members of the local church, with each person contributing according to the gifts and opportunities God has provided.

This class series, *Tools for Ministry,* is built upon the conviction that every follower of Jesus has a place in His work. Ministry is not defined by a title, position, or program; it is expressed through daily obedience, sacrificial service, and the use of God-given abilities for the good of others. When members of the body of Christ devote themselves to these practices, the church is strengthened, and the gospel is advanced.

Over the course of twelve weeks, we will explore how God equips His people for service. First, we will establish the foundation tools of ministry by learning how to handle Scripture, develop a prayer life shaped by mission, encourage one another in faith, and share the gospel in daily conversation. Next, we will turn to relational tools, considering how spiritual gifts, mentoring, burden-bearing, and hospitality provide practical avenues for service. Finally, we will look at the endurance tools that sustain ministry over the long haul—perseverance, truth joined with grace, unity, and the call to put everything together in active service.

Taken together, these lessons are intended to provide a comprehensive picture of what it means to be equipped for ministry. They move beyond theory to practice, beyond mere knowledge to application, so that by the end of the quarter each participant can identify concrete ways to serve. Our prayer is that this study will clarify the role every Christian has in God's mission and inspire deeper devotion to the work of building up the body of Christ.

How to Use This Book

This workbook is intended to help you engage with Scripture, participate meaningfully in class, and put what you learn into practice. The following suggestions will help you make the most of your study:

1. Read the Lesson in Advance

Each lesson includes a theme passage, key points, and guiding questions. Take a few minutes before class to read the Scripture text(s) and think about the lesson's focus. Note initial observations, questions, or applications that come to mind.

2. Participate in Class Discussion

The class format is designed to be interactive. Your teacher(s) will share insights, but the strength of this study lies in the contributions of the whole group. Be prepared to share what you've learned, ask questions, and encourage others.

3. Take Notes Actively

Use the space provided to write down key ideas, Scriptures, or personal applications. Writing as you listen helps you retain what you are learning and provides a record to revisit later.

4. Apply What You Learn

Each lesson concludes with practical challenges for personal ministry. Choose at least one specific step to put into practice each week. The goal of this study is not simply to gain knowledge but to cultivate habits of service that strengthen the body of Christ.

5. Reflect and Pray

Spend time after each class reflecting on how God is calling you to serve. Ask Him for wisdom, courage, and perseverance as you put these tools into use. Prayer is essential for turning lessons into lasting transformation.

6. Review the Quarter as a Whole

At the end of the study, review your notes and applications. Identify patterns of growth, areas where God has stretched you, and new opportunities for ministry. Consider sharing what you have learned with others, so that the equipping you have received can multiply further.

Part One

Foundation Tools

Every lasting work of ministry begins with strong foundations. In this section, we will examine the essential tools God has given to anchor and equip His people: Scripture, prayer, encouragement, and the sharing of faith. Scripture provides the wisdom and direction needed for every good work; prayer connects us to God's power and aligns us with His purposes; encouragement strengthens and sustains both the individual and the body; and the sharing of faith ensures that the message of Christ continues to reach the lost. Together, these practices form the core disciplines through which every Christian is equipped to serve effectively in God's kingdom.

Lesson 1

How to Read and Apply Scripture

2 Timothy 3:16–17

All Scripture is inspired by God and is profitable for teaching, for rebuking, for correcting, for training in righteousness, so that the man of God may be complete, equipped for every good work, 2 Timothy 3:16–17.

Class Overview: This opening lesson reminds us that the Bible is the essential tool God has placed in our hands for ministry. From 2 Timothy 3:16–17 we learn that Scripture is *God-breathed,* carrying His authority and life, and that it serves a vital purpose: to teach, rebuke, correct, and train us in righteousness so that we are fully equipped for every good work. Our goal is not just to read the Word but to live it—approaching it regularly, carefully, prayerfully, for application, and with others. As we begin this quarter on *Tools for Ministry,* we start with the foundation: learning to use God's Word well, so that it shapes us into servants ready to build up the body of Christ.

Class Objectives:

By the end of this class, you should be able to:

1. Understand the nature of Scripture.
2. Recognize the purposes of Scripture.
3. See the goal of Scripture.
4. Develop practical habits for Bible engagement.
5. Apply the Word personally and in ministry.

Introduction

Earlier this year, I bought a laser engraver for my business. It had everything I needed to get started—a heavy-duty table to hold the items I would engrave, a blower to get all the fumes out of my garage, and various tools that would allow me to engrave in the round. For the first few weeks, I kept everything neatly tucked away in the large crate it came trucked in with. I liked knowing I had it. But when my wife began to pressure me to get busy and learn how to use it, I realized something: owning the machine and knowing how to use it are two very different things. After I opened the crate, I stood there with everything spread out, but I didn't know what to do with half of it.

That moment has stuck with me, because it reminds me of how many of us treat the Bible. We have multiple copies sitting on our shelves. We've got apps on our phones that can access the text in dozens of translations. We may even carry it with us to church every Sunday. But having the tool is not the same as knowing how to use it. God's Word isn't meant to just sit there looking important; it's meant to equip us, to be opened, studied, and applied in real life.

Every meaningful ministry begins with a foundation in God's Word. Before we can encourage, serve, or teach others, we must first allow Scripture to shape us. Paul reminded Timothy that *all Scripture is inspired by God and is profitable for teaching, for rebuking, for correcting, for training in righteousness, so that the man of God may be complete, equipped for every good work* (2 Timothy 3:16–17). In other words, God has placed in our hands a tool that equips us not only to know Him but also to carry out the mission He has given us.

Think about it: a carpenter depends on his hammer and saw. A teacher depends on her books and lesson plans. A doctor depends on his instruments. Without the right tools, their work would be impossible. The same is true for ministry: if we want to be effective servants of Christ, we must learn how to use the tool God has given us: His Word.

This class is about moving from theory to practice. We will not just talk about the value of Scripture; we will explore how to open it, study it, and live it out. Ministry is not reserved for "professionals." Every Christian has a role to play in God's mission, and every Christian needs to be equipped. Scripture is God's equipping tool. When we learn how to read it with care, humility, and expectation, it becomes *a lamp to our feet and a light to our path* (Psalm 119:105).

So, let's begin by asking a simple but powerful question: *What role does Scripture play in your daily life?* Is it simply something you read to check off a box, or is it the guide that shapes your decisions, your relationships, and your service in Christ's kingdom? This quarter is about being equipped for ministry. And today, we start with the most essential tool of all: God's Word.

The Nature of Scripture (What It Is)

Imagine you receive two letters in the mail. One is from a stranger: maybe an advertisement or a political flyer. You glance at it, maybe toss it aside without much thought. The other is handwritten by your father or mother, or perhaps a close friend. You open it carefully, reading every line with attention, because you know the voice behind it. The difference isn't in the paper or the ink; the difference is in the author. That's exactly how we should think about the Bible. It is not junk mail from the past, nor is it a collection of random religious writings. It is the voice of our Father, the words of the living God given to us.

Paul says in 2 Timothy 3:16, *all Scripture is inspired by God.* The word "inspired" here comes from the Greek *theopneustos,* literally "God-breathed." That means the Scriptures carry the breath of God Himself. Just as God breathed life into Adam and he became a living being (Genesis 2:7), so God has breathed His life into the words of Scripture. They are alive, infused with His Spirit, and they have the power to give life and light to us.

At the same time, the Bible has a dual nature. On one level, it is clearly a human book. Moses, David, Isaiah, Luke, Paul, and others wrote with their own vocabulary, culture, and style. Yet on another level, it is fully divine. Peter explains this when he writes, *no prophecy of Scripture comes from the prophet's own interpretation, because no prophecy ever came by the will of man; instead, men spoke from God as they were carried along by the Holy Spirit* (2 Peter 1:20–21). The human authors put pen to paper, but God's Spirit directed the outcome. This makes the Bible unlike any other book in existence: fully rooted in human history, yet carrying divine authority that transcends all cultures and ages.

Because God is the source, the Scriptures are not only inspired, but they are also authoritative and trustworthy. Jesus Himself believed this. When Satan tempted him in the wilderness, His defense was not human reasoning but the Word of God: *it is written…* (Matthew 4:4, 7, 10). If the Son of God relied on Scripture to confront temptation and define truth, how much more must we? To dismiss or neglect Scripture is ultimately to ignore or neglect the God who gave it.

This is why the writer of Hebrews says, *for the word of God is living and effective and sharper than any double-edged sword, penetrating as far as the separation of soul and spirit, joints and marrow. It is able to judge the thoughts and intentions of the heart"* (Hebrews 4:12). The Bible is not a dusty relic or an outdated manual. It is alive, relevant, and piercing. It cuts through our excuses, exposes our sin, comforts our fears, and guides our steps. It is living and active because the God who breathed it out is living and active.

So, when we open the pages of Scripture, we are not merely studying history or gathering information. We are encountering the living God. His voice speaks through these words. His Spirit works through them to convict, to encourage, and to transform. That is the nature of Scripture: God-breathed, reliable, authoritative, and life-giving.

The Purpose of Scripture (What It Does)

If the nature of Scripture is that it is God-breathed, then its purpose flows directly from that truth. God did not give us His Word simply to inform us, but to transform us. Paul says in 2 Timothy 3:16 that Scripture is *profitable for teaching, for rebuking, for correcting, for training in righteousness.* These four functions describe the way the Word shapes us into the people God wants us to be.

1. Scripture teaches us.

It reveals truth about God, about the world, and about us that we could not discover on our own. The psalmist wrote, *the instruction of the Lord is perfect, renewing one's life; the testimony of the Lord is trustworthy, making the inexperienced wise* (Psalm 19:7). Teaching here is not just about information; it's about direction. Scripture gives us the wisdom to know what is right, what pleases God, and how to walk in His ways.

2. Scripture rebukes us.

This is not always comfortable, but it is essential. God's Word exposes the lies we believe and the sins we commit. Hebrews 4:12 reminds us that the Word judges the thoughts and intentions of the heart. When we read the Bible honestly, it holds up a mirror to our lives, confronting the places where we fall short of God's will. Sometimes that sting of rebuke is exactly what keeps us from drifting further into sin.

3. Scripture corrects us.

Rebuke shows us where we are wrong, but correction puts us back on the right path. It's like a GPS that not only tells you when you've made a wrong turn but reroutes you toward your destination. God doesn't just expose sin to condemn us; He shows us the better way to live. David prayed, *show me the way I should go, because I appeal to you* (Psalm 143:8). Scripture provides that guidance, helping us realign with God's will.

4. Scripture trains us in righteousness.

This is more than a quick fix; it's about long-term training. Training implies discipline, repetition, and practice. Just as an athlete trains daily to grow stronger, Christians immerse themselves in the Word so that over time their character, attitudes, and actions are shaped into Christlikeness. Paul urged Timothy, *train yourself in godliness. For the training of the body has limited benefit, but godliness is beneficial in every way* (1 Timothy 4:7–8). Training through the Word builds habits of holiness and equips us to live faithfully in every situation.

Taken together, these purposes of Scripture show us that the Bible is not passive. It is very active. It is God's instrument for growth. It instructs, convicts, redirects, and forms us. And just as a skilled craftsman uses his tools to shape wood or metal into something beautiful and useful, so God uses His Word to shape us into the likeness of His Son.

The Goal of Scripture (What it Produces)

If Scripture is God-breathed and profitable for teaching, rebuking, correcting, and training, then what is the ultimate goal? Paul answers in 2 Timothy 3:17: *"So that the man of God may be complete, equipped for every good work."* God's Word is not just about information or even transformation on a personal level; its ultimate purpose is equipping us for ministry.

1. It leads to maturity.

The word "complete" means mature, whole, or fully developed. God's desire is not that we remain spiritual infants, dependent on others for every answer, but that we grow up into Christ (Ephesians 4:13–15). The Scriptures provide everything we need for that growth. They give us a foundation of truth, a guide for living, and a training ground for discernment, so that we can be strong and steady in our faith.

2. It inspires good works.

But Paul does not stop at maturity. He adds that Scripture equips us for *every good work*. In other words, the Bible is not just meant to make us better Bible students; it is meant to make us better servants. The Word prepares us to live out our calling in real and practical ways: to encourage the discouraged, to stand firm in trials, to serve others with love, to share the gospel with boldness. It equips us not simply to know about ministry, but to do ministry.

James reminds us, *"Be doers of the word and not hearers only, deceiving yourselves"* (James 1:22). It is possible to know the Bible well, to memorize verses, even to teach others, and yet fail to apply it. But the true goal of Scripture is not just knowledge; it is obedience. It produces people who act on what they believe. The evidence that God's Word has taken root in us is seen not only in what we can recite but in how we live.

For example, a soldier does not spend months in training to say he has been trained; he does it to be ready for the mission. In the same way, Scripture equips us to be prepared for the work God puts before us, big or small, public or private, visible or unseen. When we let the Word do its work, we are prepared, mature, and able to serve in ways that bring glory to Christ.

How Do We use it Well?

We've seen what Scripture is and what it does, but the next question is: how do we use it well? Many Christians struggle not because they don't believe the Bible, but because they don't know how to bridge the gap between reading and living. Here are five practical steps to help us do just that:

1. **Read Regularly**
   Just as our bodies need daily bread, our souls need daily Scripture (Matthew 4:4). Sporadic reading leads to shallow growth. Make Bible intake a rhythm; whether first thing in the morning, during a lunch break, or before bed. Consistency matters more than quantity. Start small if needed, but start often.
2. **Read Carefully**
   Context matters. Ask: Who is speaking? Who is addressed? What is the situation? Misunderstanding often comes when we lift verses out of their setting. Careful reading helps us see not just words but meaning. Like the Bereans in Acts 17:11, we should examine the Scriptures daily, thoughtfully testing what we hear and read.
3. **Read Prayerfully**
   The Bible is not just a book to study; it is a conversation with the living God. Before opening the Word, ask Him: *Open my eyes so that I may contemplate wondrous things from your instruction* (Psalm 119:18). Invite the Spirit to give clarity, conviction, and comfort. Reading prayerfully reminds us that Scripture is living and personal, not abstract.
4. **Read for Application**
   Every passage raises questions we must answer: What does this teach me about God? What does this reveal about myself? What does God want me to do in light of this truth? Application moves us from theory to practice. James 1:25 describes the blessed person as the one who looks intently into the Word, perseveres in it, and *does it.*
5. **Read and Study with Others**
   We were never meant to journey through Scripture alone. Studying together sharpens our understanding and holds us accountable. Proverbs 27:17 reminds us, *Iron sharpens iron, and one person sharpens another.* Share insights with family, friends, or your church group. Hearing how others apply the Word can inspire and challenge us to do the same.

Challenge

This week, pick one passage of Scripture and walk through these five steps. Read it regularly for several days, pay attention to the context, pray for understanding, write down at least one personal application, and share it with someone else.

Conclusion

The Bible is not just another book on our shelves. It is the very breath of God, living and active, given to equip us for every good work. We've seen today that its nature is divine, its purpose is to teach, rebuke, correct, and train, and its goal is to make us complete and ready to serve. Scripture is not about filling our heads with knowledge but about shaping our hearts and hands for ministry.

But here's the critical question: What will we do with it? Owning a Bible is not enough. Quoting verses is not enough. Even admiring the wisdom of Scripture is not enough. God calls us to read it, to believe it, and most importantly, to live it. James warns us not to be hearers only, deceiving ourselves, but to be doers of the Word (James 1:22). Real equipping happens when the truth of Scripture moves off the page and into our daily lives.

So, as we begin this quarter on *Tools for Ministry,* remember that every other tool we will study, prayer, encouragement, discipleship, hospitality, perseverance, depends on this one. The Word of God is the foundation of all ministry. If we use it well, it will shape us, strengthen us, and send us into the world ready to serve.

This week, take one passage and put it into practice. Let the Word correct you where you need correction, encourage you where you need hope, and equip you where you need strength. And as you do, remember that every time you open your Bible, you are hearing the voice of your Father, who has breathed His very life into these words for your good and His glory.

For Discussion

1. Think about the story of my unused laser engraver. In what ways do we sometimes treat the Bible, owning it but not using it?

    ____
    ____
    ____

2. What difference does it make to you personally that Scripture is "God-breathed" (2 Tim. 3:16)? How does that truth shape the way we should approach reading it?

    ____
    ____
    ____

3. Of the four functions Paul lists, teaching, rebuking, correcting, training, which one do you find the easiest to accept? Which one is the hardest? Why?

    ____
    ____
    ____

4. Can you share a time when Scripture corrected you, encouraged you, or equipped you for something specific in life or ministry?

    ____
    ____
    ____

5. We talked about reading regularly, carefully, prayerfully, for application, and together with others. Which of these practices do you already do well? Which do you need to grow in?

    ____
    ____
    ____

6. If the goal of Scripture is to equip us for ministry, what is one "good work" you feel more prepared to do because of your time in the Word?

    ____
    ____
    ____

Lesson 2

How to Pray for Ministry

Ephesians 6:18–20

Pray at all times in the Spirit with every prayer and request, and stay alert with all perseverance and intercession for all the saints. Pray also for me, that the message may be given to me when I open my mouth to make known with boldness the mystery of the gospel. For this I am an ambassador in chains. Pray that I might be bold enough to speak about it as I should,

Hebrews 11:8–16.

Class Overview: This lesson emphasizes that prayer is not just a private devotion but the lifeblood of ministry. From Ephesians 6:18–20, we see that prayer expresses our constant dependence on God, our intercession for fellow believers, and our need for boldness to proclaim the gospel. Just as Scripture equips us for good works, prayer empowers us to carry them out. Ministry without prayer becomes self-reliant and weak, but when we pray in the Spirit, we invite God's strength, wisdom, and courage into our service. This class will challenge us to move beyond routine prayers to intentional, ministry-shaped prayer that sustains, unites, and emboldens the people of God.

Class Objectives:

By the end of this class, you should be able to:

1. Explain why prayer is essential to the life of a Christian and to the work of ministry, based on Ephesians 6:18–20.
2. Describe what it means to "pray at all times in the Spirit" and identify practical ways to build continual prayer into daily life.
3. Learn how to pray not only for personal needs but also for fellow believers, leaders, and ministries, following Paul's example.
4. Understand that courage in sharing the gospel comes through prayer, and commit to praying for boldness in personal ministry opportunities.
5. Apply specific practices such as keeping a ministry prayer list,

praying Scripture, and praying with others to strengthen individual and congregational ministry.
6. Choose one specific ministry situation and commit it to daily prayer throughout the week, looking for ways God answers.

Introduction

I SIT IN A LOT OF MEETINGS. Hours are poured into planning: scheduling events, building class objectives, and planning out lesson series. One of the things I appreciate about our shepherds is their dedication to prayer. One of them will usually say something like this before things get going: "Before we do anything, we need to spend time in prayer." We pray for God to go before us, for the Spirit to work on honest hearts, and for the courage to speak and lead. That opening prayer often changes the entire tone of the meeting. The plans we make are helpful, but the power comes when we put the work in God's hands. Conversations open up that were never expected. Opportunities unfold that we hadn't planned for. The difference isn't our preparation; it is God's provision, accessed through prayer.

Prayer is not a formality before ministry; it is the lifeblood of ministry. Without prayer, even our best efforts are limited to human strength. With prayer, we invite the power of God into our work. That's why Paul, after describing the armor of God in Ephesians 6, immediately says, *Pray at all times in the Spirit with every prayer and request, and stay alert with all perseverance and intercession for all the saints* (Ephesians 6:18). Prayer is not just something we do before the battle; it is part of the battle. It is how we stay connected to the Commander and receive strength for the fight.

Think about it: Jesus Himself lived this truth. Before choosing the twelve apostles, He spent the whole night in prayer (Luke 6:12). Before facing the cross, He poured out His heart in Gethsemane, submitting His will to the Father (Matthew 26:36–39). If the Son of God needed prayer to sustain Him in ministry, how much more do we?

As we studied previously, Scripture is the tool God places in our hands to equip us. But prayer is what keeps us connected to the One who gives that tool its power. Prayer is dependence. Prayer is surrender. Prayer is the ongoing reminder that ministry is not about what we can do for God, but about what God can do through us.

So, as we begin this lesson, let's ask ourselves an honest question: *When it comes to ministry, am I leaning more on my plans, or on God's power?*

Prayer as Constant Dependence

1. At all times.

Paul begins this section by urging believers to *pray at all times in the Spirit with every prayer and request* (Ephesians 6:18a). The phrase "at all times" reminds us that prayer is not meant to be an occasional act but a continual posture. Just as breathing is constant for physical life, prayer is constant for spiritual life. A ministry that is not rooted in prayer quickly becomes self-driven and fragile.

2. In the Spirit.

The key phrase here is *in the Spirit.* Paul is not simply commanding us to pray often but to pray in step with the Spirit of God. Romans 8:26–27 tells us that the Spirit helps us in our weakness, even interceding for us when we do not know how to pray. That means prayer is more than us bringing requests; it is the Spirit shaping our hearts and aligning us with God's will.

Think of a soldier on the battlefield. No matter how strong or skilled he is, he cannot fight alone. He needs constant communication with his commander. If the line of communication is cut, he quickly becomes vulnerable. That's the picture Paul is painting. Prayer is our line of communication with God, our source of wisdom, strength, and direction. When we pray at all times in the Spirit, we are refusing to fight in our own power, we are drawing from the limitless resources of God.

3. Practical implications.

Praying always doesn't mean we are always on our knees with eyes closed. It means we live with a continual awareness of God's presence, lifting up situations to Him throughout the day. It means beginning ministry tasks with prayer, whether that's teaching a class, visiting a sick friend, or serving a meal. It means pausing to ask for God's wisdom before answering a tough question. It means seeing prayer as our first response, not our last resort.

When we live in constant dependence through prayer, we acknowledge that ministry is not about what we can accomplish for God, but about what God can accomplish through us. As Jesus said in John 15:5, *"Apart from me you can do nothing."* Prayer keeps us connected to the Vine so that our ministry bears fruit.

Prayer as Intercession

Paul continues in Ephesians 6:18, *With every prayer and request, stay alert with all perseverance and intercession for all the saints.* Here, the focus shifts outward. Prayer is not only about our own dependence on God but also about lifting up others before His throne. Ministry is a team effort, and prayer is the glue that holds the team together.

Notice Paul's emphasis on "all perseverance and intercession for all the saints." This is not casual or occasional prayer; it is steady, persistent, ongoing prayer for others in the body of Christ. Ministry is never just about "me and God"; it is about "us and God." We are called to carry one another's burdens (Galatians 6:2), and one of the primary ways we do that is through prayer.

Consider how different the church would be if our first instinct when hearing about someone's struggles was to pray. Not just to promise prayer but to actually stop and do it. When Paul writes to the Colossians, he says, *we haven't stopped praying for you. We are asking that you may be filled with the knowledge of his will in all wisdom and spiritual understanding, so that you may walk worthy of the Lord* (Colossians 1:9–10). Paul's intercession teaches us how to pray: not only for relief from problems but for growth, strength, and fruitfulness in ministry.

Imagine a soldier on the battlefield who not only fights for himself but also keeps watch over his comrades. He notices when someone is weak or exposed, and he calls for support. That's the essence of intercessory prayer. It's looking out for others, asking God to strengthen them when they are vulnerable, and celebrating when they stand firm.

In practice, this means our prayers should go beyond just health and physical needs (though those matter) to include spiritual concerns: boldness, perseverance, wisdom, faith, and fruitfulness in ministry. It involves developing the habit of asking others, "How can I pray for you in your service to God this week?" It also includes lifting up leaders, teachers, parents, new Christians, and even those who are struggling, so that no one in the body fights alone.

When we pray for each other in this way, we not only help carry one another's burdens but also knit our hearts together in love. Intercession strengthens unity, deepens compassion, and reminds us that ministry is not a solo mission; it's the entire body working together through God's power.

Prayer as Boldness for the Gospel

After calling us to constant dependence and intercession, Paul makes a personal request: *Pray also for me, that the message may be given to me when I open my mouth to make known with boldness the mystery of the gospel. For this I am an ambassador in chains. Pray that I might be bold enough to speak about it as I should* (Ephesians 6:19–20).

It is striking that Paul, the seasoned apostle who had preached on three missionary journeys, planted churches across the Roman world, and endured countless hardships for Christ, still asks for prayer. And not just any prayer; he asks specifically for boldness. If Paul needed courage to speak, how much more do we?

Paul's request reminds us that proclaiming the gospel is not just a matter of skill, knowledge, or personality. It requires divine help. Fear is natural. Rejection is painful. Opposition is real. But boldness comes when we lean on God through prayer. The early church understood this well. In Acts 4, after the authorities threatened Peter and John, the believers prayed, *Lord, consider their threats, and grant that your servants may speak your word with all boldness* (Acts 4:29). The result? *They were all filled with the Holy Spirit and began to speak the word of God boldly* (Acts 4:31).

Think of it this way: boldness is not the absence of fear, but the presence of faith. Prayer transforms fear into courage because it reminds us that the power of the gospel does not rest on us, but on God. When we pray for boldness, we are not asking to become fearless; we are asking for the strength to be faithful despite fear.

In practice, this means our prayers for ministry should not only focus on open doors but also on the courage to walk through them. We may pray for opportunities to invite a neighbor to worship, for wisdom to answer a friend's questions, or for courage to stand firm at work or school when our faith is challenged. Boldness is needed not only in pulpits and mission fields but also in kitchens, classrooms, and office cubicles. Wherever the gospel needs to be spoken, prayer for boldness must precede it.

Paul's example demonstrates the humility of even the greatest servant of Christ; he recognized he could not do it alone. He asked his brothers and sisters to support him with prayer so that the mystery of Christ could be clearly and fearlessly proclaimed. That same call still resonates with us today. We need to be people who pray not only for health, safety, and provision but also for the courage to speak and live out the gospel as we should.

Practical Application: How to Pray for Ministry

We've seen that prayer is our lifeline to God. It expresses our dependence, lifts up others, and gives us boldness to share the gospel. But how do we put this into practice? Here are several simple yet powerful ways:

1. **Start Every Ministry with Prayer**
   Before teaching a class, visiting a friend, serving at a meal, or stepping into a difficult conversation, pause to pray. Ask God for wisdom, love, and strength. Prayer re-centers us on His power, not ours.
2. **Create a Ministry Prayer List**
   Go beyond physical needs. Write down the names of people you are trying to reach with the gospel, ministries you serve in, leaders in your congregation, and fellow Christians who are struggling. Make it a habit to lift these regularly before God.

3. **Pray Scripture Back to God**
   Use passages like Ephesians 6:18–20, Colossians 4:2–4, or Acts 4:29–31 as templates for your prayers. When we pray God's Word, we align our requests with His will and promises.
4. **Pray with Others, Not Just Alone**
   Prayer meetings, small groups, or even a quick phone call with a friend can strengthen ministry. Interceding together deepens fellowship and multiplies encouragement. Remember, Paul didn't just pray; he asked others to pray for him.
5. **Pray Specifically for Boldness**
   Instead of only praying for "open doors," pray for courage to walk through them when God opens the way. Ask God for clarity in your words and faithfulness in your actions, even when it's difficult.

Challenge

This week, commit to praying daily for one specific ministry situation in your life. Ask God for strength to serve, for someone else to be encouraged, or for boldness to share the gospel. Write it down, pray over it consistently, and look for how God answers.

Conclusion

Prayer is not an accessory to ministry; it is the lifeline of ministry. Paul reminds us in Ephesians 6:18–20 that prayer is constant dependence on God, intercession for one another, and a plea for boldness to proclaim the gospel. Without prayer, even the most gifted servant quickly runs out of strength. But with prayer, ordinary Christians are empowered to do extraordinary work, because God Himself supplies what is needed.

We saw in Lesson 1 that Scripture equips us for every good work. Prayer now shows us how those works are carried out: not in our own power, but in God's. Ministry is never about what we can accomplish for Him, but about what He can accomplish through us. Prayer keeps us humble, united, and courageous.

So here is the challenge: let's not just talk about prayer for ministry, let's practice it. This week, choose one ministry situation, a person you're reaching out to, a work you're serving in, or a fear you're facing, and commit it to prayer every day. Pray for yourself, for your brothers and sisters, and for boldness to act. And then watch as God takes our weakness and uses it for His glory.

For Discussion

1. Think back to the story in the introduction. Why do you think we are sometimes tempted to rush into ministry without pausing to pray first?

   ___

   ___

   ___

2. What does it mean to "pray at all times in the Spirit"? How can we develop a habit of prayer that feels natural and constant rather than forced or occasional?

   ___

   ___

   ___

3. When you think about your own prayer life, how much of it is focused on your needs versus the needs of others? What are some specific ways we can grow in interceding for fellow Christians?

   ___

   ___

   ___

4. Paul, a seasoned apostle, still asked others to pray for his boldness. What does that teach us about our own need for prayer in evangelism? Can you recall a time when prayer gave you courage to speak when you were afraid?

   ___

   ___

   ___

5. Which of the five practices from the application section (start every ministry with prayer, prayer lists, praying Scripture, praying with others, praying for boldness) do you find most helpful? Which one would you like to begin practicing this week

___

___

___

6. If you were to commit to praying daily this week for one ministry situation in your life, what would it be? How might sharing that commitment with others help you stay faithful to it?

___

___

___

Lesson 3

How to Encourage and Build Up

Hebrews 10:24–25

And let us consider one another in order to provoke love and good works, not neglecting to gather together, as some are in the habit of doing, but encouraging each other, and all the more as you see the day approaching, Hebrews 10:24–25.

Class Overview: Encouragement is one of the simplest yet most powerful ministries available to every Christian. From Hebrews 10:24–25 we learn that encouragement requires intentionality, presence, and urgency. By considering one another, we stir each other up to love and good works. By gathering together, we strengthen one another through our presence. And as the Day of Christ draws near, encouragement becomes increasingly vital to help us endure trials and resist discouragement. This lesson reminds us that encouragement is not optional—it is essential—and challenges us to use words, presence, and actions to build up the body of Christ.

Class Objectives:

By the end of this class, you should be able to:

1. Explain what it means to "consider one another" (Heb. 10:24) and how encouragement stirs others toward love and good works.
2. Describe why gathering together is essential for encouragement and how our presence strengthens the body.
3. Understand why encouragement becomes "all the more" important as trials increase and the Day of Christ approaches.
4. Commit to specific practices such as speaking words of grace, showing up intentionally, and recognizing silent struggles.
5. Take the class challenge to encourage at least three people this week—one with words, one with presence, and one with action.

Introduction

I'll never forget a Sunday years ago when I was feeling especially worn down. The week before had been heavy, full of problems, criticism, and discouragement. I preached that morning, but afterward I felt like I had missed the mark. *You can't knock it out of the park with every sermon* ... As I stood near the back, one of my older sisters came up, put her hand on my shoulder, and said, "You have no idea how much I needed that lesson today. God used you to speak right into my heart." Her words lifted a weight off me that I had been carrying all week. They reminded me that God was working, even when I couldn't see it. That five-second moment of encouragement fueled me for days to come.

All of us can recall times when a word of encouragement made a huge difference. It might have been a note in the mail during a tough time. Or a visit at the hospital. Perhaps it was a hug or a smile when you felt unseen. Encouragement is powerful. It doesn't cost much, but it can mean everything to the person who receives it.

The Hebrew writer knew this, which is why he urged Christians, *,et us consider one another in order to provoke love and good works, not neglecting to gather together, as some are in the habit of doing, but encouraging each other, and all the more as you see the Day approaching* (Hebrews 10:24–25). In a world where Christians were facing persecution and temptation to give up, encouragement was not just a nice gesture: it was a lifeline.

Today, it's no different. We live in a culture filled with criticism, negativity, and loneliness. Many people come into our assemblies carrying burdens we can't see. They may be one word of encouragement away from holding on ... or giving up. As followers of Christ, one of the most powerful tools we have for ministry is not a sermon, a class, or a program. It is encouragement: showing up, speaking life, and building up others in faith.

So, here's the question we'll explore in this lesson: *How can we be intentional encouragers who strengthen the body of Christ and help one another endure until the Day of Christ?*

The Call to Encourage

The Hebrew writer begins with this exhortation: *let us consider one another in order to provoke love and good works* (Hebrews 10:24). Notice the phrase "let us consider." Encouragement is not accidental; it is intentional. It requires us to slow down and think carefully about the needs of others. The word *consider* means to fix your attention on, to study closely. In other words, the writer is saying: Don't just think about yourself; take time to notice the people around you.

Encouragement begins when we choose to look beyond our own world. That means asking: Who here is struggling? Who here looks weary? Who here needs to be reminded of God's love? If we never stop to consider others, we will miss countless opportunities to build them up. Paul expressed the same idea in Philippians 2:4, *everyone should look not to his own interests, but rather to the interests of others.* Encouragement starts with eyes that see.

But the writer goes further. He says our purpose is to "provoke" or "stir up" one another to love and good works. The word literally means to *sharpen* or to *stimulate.* Just as iron sharpens iron (Proverbs 27:17), our encouragement should stir something in others, motivating them to love more deeply and to serve more faithfully. Encouragement is not flattery or vague kindness; it is purposeful, aiming to strengthen faith and inspire action.

A coach on the sidelines doesn't just cheer to make the players feel good; he cheers to push them forward into action. In the same way, our encouragement should not just soothe feelings but should inspire growth. True encouragement doesn't leave people where they are … it helps them take the next step.

Practically, this means encouragement requires intentionality. It's more than saying, "Good job." It might be telling a young Christian, "I see your faith growing, and it encourages me." It might be telling a tired parent, "Your example of bringing your kids to worship week after week is a blessing to us all." It might be sending a message to a teacher, "Thank you for the way you pour into your class; it makes a difference." These words don't just affirm ... they stir up. They remind others that their efforts matter and that God is using them.

When we answer this call to encourage, we begin to create a culture of love and service in the church. Encouragement is contagious. One word or act can ripple outward, inspiring others to step forward in faith and good works. That's the power of intentional encouragement.

The Power of Presence

The Hebrew writer continues: *not neglecting to gather together, as some are in the habit of doing, but encouraging each other* (Hebrews 10:25). Here we see that encouragement is not just about words ... It's about presence. Our very act of showing up together is a form of encouragement.

The early Christians lived in a hostile world. Some had already begun slipping away from the assemblies, either from fear of persecution or from spiritual weariness. The writer reminds them that neglecting the gathering weakens not only their own faith but also the faith of others. When we are absent, the body feels it. When we are present, the body is strengthened.

Sometimes, the best encouragement you can give is simply showing up. Words may not always come easily, but presence speaks volumes. Think of how comforting it is when a friend visits the hospital, not to say much, but just to sit by your side. Or when someone consistently attends worship, even during personal hardship; their very presence demonstrates their trust in God and encourages others to keep going.

Paul understood this power. Writing to the Romans, he said, *I want very much to see you, so that I may impart to you some spiritual gift to strengthen you, that is, to be mutually encouraged by each other's faith, both yours and mine* (Romans 1:11–12). Notice that phrase: *mutually encouraged.* Our presence with one another builds up both sides.

Practically, this means our gathering is not just about what we *get* but about what we *give.* When you come to worship, you bring encouragement with you. Your singing, your participation, your conversations before and after ... these are all ways God uses you to strengthen others. When you stay home, the church loses a piece of its encouragement.

So how do we put this into practice? Aim not only to be physically present but also genuinely *engaged.* Don't arrive late and leave early without making connections. Look around the room: Who needs a handshake, a smile, or a kind word? Who could use someone sitting beside them? Don't underestimate the power of showing up. God uses your presence to encourage others.

The Urgency of Encouragement

The Hebrew writer concludes this exhortation with a sense of urgency—*and all the more as you see the Day approaching* (Hebrews 10:25b). He reminds us that encouragement is not just important … it is increasingly necessary as time moves forward.

The "Day" here likely points to the return of Christ, but the principle applies even now: as trials increase, as pressures mount, and as faith is tested, the need for encouragement only grows. The closer we get to eternity, the more critical it is to hold each other up. We cannot afford to let one another drift, because the stakes are eternal.

Encouragement is not a "once in a while" gesture; it is a daily necessity. Hebrews 3:13 says, *but encourage each other daily, while it is still called today, so that none of you is hardened by sin's deception.* Notice the warning: without encouragement, hearts grow hard. Sin is deceitful, suffering is draining, and Satan is relentless. That's why encouragement is urgent; it keeps us tender, faithful, and focused on the hope before us.

Think of a runner in a marathon. By mile 20, exhaustion sets in. Muscles ache, lungs burn, and the temptation to quit is strong. Then a crowd of supporters lines the road, clapping and shouting, "Keep going! You can do this!" That encouragement doesn't remove the pain, but it gives strength to endure. That is what the Hebrew writer is calling for: a community of church members cheering one another on as we press toward the finish line.

For us, this means we cannot assume that people are "fine." Many around us are barely holding on. Some sit in our pews smiling outwardly while silently struggling. A simple act of encouragement: a note, a text, a visit, a prayer, might be the very thing that keeps their faith alive another day. That's why we must encourage "all the more."

The urgency is clear: time is short, struggles are real, and the Day is coming. Encouragement is not optional; it is essential. And the church that takes this seriously will be a place where no one walks alone, where every believer is strengthened, and where together we endure until Christ returns.

Practical Application: How to Encourage and Build Up

Encouragement is not complicated, but it does require intentionality. Hebrews 10:24–25 calls us to consider, to gather, and to encourage "all the more." Here are practical ways to live that out:

1. **Speak Life, Not Criticism**
   Paul writes, *No foul language should come from your mouth, but only what is good for building up someone in need, so that it gives grace to those who hear* (Ephesians 4:29). Make it a practice to replace complaints with words of grace. Ask yourself, *Will my words build up or tear down?*
2. **Show Up Intentionally**
   Don't underestimate the ministry of presence. Attend worship faithfully, arrive ready to engage, and look for someone who needs encouragement. A handshake, a smile, or a short conversation can mean more than you realize.
3. **Practice Daily Encouragement**
   Hebrews 3:13 calls us to encourage *daily.* This could be as simple as sending a text, writing a note, or offering a prayer for someone each day. Small acts, repeated consistently, create a culture of encouragement.
4. **Recognize Silent Struggles**
   Be sensitive to those who may not voice their needs. A quiet person in the pew, a young Christian, a weary parent, or someone who hasn't been present for a while; these are often the ones who need encouragement most. Take the initiative to reach out.

5. **Stir, Don't Just Soothe**
   Remember that encouragement is not only comfort; it's also motivation. Think about how you can stir others to greater love and good works. Instead of just saying, "You're doing great," you might say, "Your example of service inspires me—keep it up!"

Challenge

This week, choose three people to encourage in specific ways: one with words, one with presence, and one with action. Be intentional. Write their names down, follow through, and watch how God uses your encouragement to strengthen the body.

Conclusion

Encouragement may seem small, but Scripture reminds us it is one of the most powerful tools God has given His people. Hebrews 10:24–25 calls us to consider one another, to be present with one another, and to encourage one another all the more as the Day of Christ draws near. We've seen that encouragement requires intentional thoughtfulness, that our very presence strengthens others, and that the urgency of encouragement grows as trials increase and eternity draws closer.

The truth is, none of us make it to heaven alone. We need one another. We need to be stirred up to love and good works, reminded that we are not forgotten, and strengthened to endure. Encouragement is not optional for Christians. It is essential for the health of the body and the endurance of the saints.

So, the challenge for us is simple but profound: don't leave encouragement to chance. Be intentional. This week, ask God to open your eyes to someone who needs a kind word, a visit, or a helping hand. Remember that your encouragement may be the very thing that helps a brother or sister keep pressing on in faith. And as we make encouragement a way of life, the church will become the place God designed it to be: a place of hope, love, and strength until the Day we see Christ face to face.

For Discussion

1. Can you share a time when someone's encouragement made a significant difference in your life? What did that moment teach you about the power of encouragement?

   ____

2. The Hebrew writer says, *"Let us consider one another."* What does it look like in practice to "consider" others? How can we train ourselves to notice the needs around us?

3. Why do you think the writer connects encouragement to gathering together? How does our presence at worship and other gatherings encourage others, even without words?

4. Why do you think encouragement becomes "all the more" important as we see the Day approaching? How does encouragement help us endure trials and resist sin's deception?

5. Of the five applications we discussed (speaking life, showing up, practicing daily encouragement, recognizing silent struggles, stirring not just soothing), which one stands out most to you? Which could you start practicing this week?

6. The challenge this week is to encourage three people in specific ways—with words, with presence, and with action. Who might God be putting on your heart right now for this assignment?

____

____

____

Lesson 4

How to Share Your Faith

1 Peter 3:15; Colossians 4:5–6

But in your hearts regard Christ the Lord as holy, ready at any time to give a defense to anyone who asks you for a reason for the hope that is in you, 1 Peter 3:15.

Act wisely toward outsiders, making the most of the time. Let your speech always be gracious, seasoned with salt, so that you may know how you should answer each person, Colossians 4:5–6.

Class Overview: Ministry is carried out in community. God has designed His people to serve and grow together, using their gifts in harmony with one another. In this section, we will explore the relational tools that enable believers to build strong spiritual connections: serving with our gifts, mentoring and being mentored, bearing one another's burdens, and practicing hospitality. These tools remind us that ministry is not an isolated effort but a shared calling in which we help one another grow in faith, maturity, and love.

Class Objectives:

By the end of this class, you should be able to:

1. Explain what it means to "be ready to give an answer" (1 Pet. 3:15) and identify practical ways to prepare a personal testimony of faith.
2. Describe how walking wisely toward outsiders (Col. 4:5) strengthens credibility and creates opportunities for gospel conversations.
3. Understand why our words must be gracious and seasoned with salt (Col. 4:6) and how tone and clarity impact gospel witness
4. Commit to simple, repeatable practices such as praying for specific people, sharing short faith stories, and weaving Scripture into everyday life.
5. Identify one person in their personal circle to pray for and seek opportunities to share their faith with during the coming week.

Introduction

YEARS AGO, I DROVE A SCHOOL BUS for a school district in South Dakota. I often drove students to extracurricular activities—many of them hundreds of miles from Rapid City. I remember a conversation I had years ago with a fellow driver during a lunch on a field trip in Wyoming. We weren't talking about religion at first, just about life, family, and the struggles we were both facing. At one point, he looked at me and said, "You always seem calm, even when things are hard. How do you do that?" In that moment, I realized God had opened a door. I didn't launch into a sermon. I said, "It's my faith in and relationship with Christ. He gives me peace when I couldn't find it on my own." That short response led to more questions, and eventually to a Bible study. It all started with a small, everyday conversation.

Many of us feel intimidated when we hear the word *evangelism.* We picture knocking on strangers' doors, debating theology, or delivering a flawless gospel presentation. But the truth is, most opportunities to share Jesus don't come in formal settings. They come in ordinary moments ... in a break room, at the ball field, on the phone with a friend, or over a cup of coffee. Evangelism isn't about having every answer; it's about pointing people to the hope you've found in Christ.

That's exactly what Peter writes in 1 Peter 3:15: *In your hearts regard Christ the Lord as holy, ready at any time to give a defense to anyone who asks you for a reason for the hope that is in you.* Sharing our faith begins with honoring Christ in our hearts and being ready to explain why we live with hope. It's not about winning arguments; it's about giving testimony.

Paul echoes this in Colossians 4:5–6, where he urges believers to act wisely toward outsiders, making the most of every opportunity, and to let their speech always be gracious and seasoned with salt. In other words, our lives and our words are meant to work together to point others to Jesus.

So, here's the challenge we'll explore in this lesson: *How can ordinary Christians, people like you and me, learn to live wisely, speak graciously, and be ready to share the hope of Christ with the people God has already placed in our lives?*

Be Ready to Give an Answer

Peter writes, *in your hearts regard Christ the Lord as holy, ready at any time to give a defense to anyone who asks you for a reason for the hope that is in you.* Notice where he begins: in the heart. Sharing our faith doesn't start with arguments or techniques; it begins with a heart that has set apart Christ as Lord. When Christ rules in our hearts, hope naturally overflows. And when hope overflows, people notice.

The command is to "be ready." That doesn't mean we must know everything, but it does mean we should be prepared to explain why Christ makes the difference in our lives. Readiness is about expectation: expecting that someone, at some point, will ask, "Why are you different?" and being willing to answer.

Peter says we are giving a "defense," not in the sense of defending ourselves in a courtroom, but in the sense of offering a reasoned explanation. The gospel is not a vague feeling; it is rooted in truth. Paul summarizes it clearly in 1 Corinthians 15:3–4: *Christ died for our sins according to the Scriptures, that He was buried, that He was raised on the third day according to the Scriptures.* Being ready means that we can articulate that core truth and explain why it gives us hope.

Imagine someone asks you about your favorite restaurant. You don't need a script. You don't need training. You share your experience, what you love about it, why you go there, and what it means to you. That's what it looks like to share your faith. You don't have to have a Ph.D. in theology to tell someone what Jesus has done in your life. You need honesty and readiness.

Practically, this means we should think ahead. How would you explain your faith in two or three sentences? Could you share, in simple terms, why you follow Jesus, what He has done for you, and the hope you have because of Him? Having that "faith story" prepared helps you feel confident when opportunities arise. It's not about being polished, it's about being personal.

Being ready also means being prayerful. We should pray daily for open doors and for the awareness to recognize them. Too often, opportunities pass by simply because we weren't looking for them. But when we live with Christ set apart in our hearts, we begin to see conversations not as coincidences but as divine appointments.

So, the call of 1 Peter 3:15 is simple: Honor Christ in your heart. Be ready to share why you have hope. And when the door opens, step through it with humility and confidence, pointing people to Jesus.

Walk in Wisdom Toward Outsiders

Paul writes, *act wisely toward outsiders, making the most of the time.* Sharing our faith is not only about what we say, but also about how we live. Our daily conduct either builds credibility for the gospel or undermines it. Evangelism is not just an event; it is a lifestyle of wisdom lived out before those who don't yet know Christ.

To "act wisely" means to live thoughtfully and intentionally. It means recognizing that unbelievers are watching, and our behavior shapes their perception of Jesus. Jesus said in Matthew 5:16, *let your light shine before others, so that they may see your good works and give glory to your Father in heaven.* Our kindness, honesty, patience, and integrity become a living testimony.

Paul adds, *making the most of the time.* The idea here is of buying up opportunities, like a wise merchant who seizes every deal. Time is short. Opportunities are fleeting. If we aren't alert, we can miss the chance to speak into someone's life. Wisdom looks for those moments, a conversation in the break room, a neighbor struggling with loss, a friend asking for advice, and recognizes them as open doors for the gospel.

Think of it like gardening. A farmer knows when the soil is ready and the season is right. He doesn't waste time; he plants. If he delays, the opportunity passes. In the same way, wise Christians learn to recognize when hearts are open and moments are ripe, and they act with urgency.

Practically, this means two things: First, *we must live consistently.* Hypocrisy closes doors faster than anything else. If our words about Christ are not backed up by lives that reflect Him, people will not listen. Second, *we must live attentively.* Each day brings small opportunities: conversations, questions, moments of kindness. Sharing our faith often begins not with a sermon but with a simple act of love that opens the door for words.

Walking in wisdom means we live in such a way that people see Jesus in us before they ever hear about Jesus from us. Our lives become the first testimony, and our words become the explanation.

Speak with Grace and Clarity

Paul continues, *let your speech always be gracious, seasoned with salt, so that you may know how you should answer each person.* If the previous section emphasized how we live, this section emphasizes how we speak. Both matter. Our conduct opens the door, but our words point people to Christ once the door is open.

Paul says our words should be *gracious.* That means marked by kindness, humility, and gentleness. Sharing our faith is never about winning arguments or proving someone wrong, it is about pointing someone to Jesus. 1 Peter 3:15 makes this clear when it adds that we must give our defense *with gentleness and respect.* People are rarely argued into the kingdom, but grace-filled conversations often draw them.

He also says our words should be *seasoned with salt.* Salt in the ancient world preserved food and enhanced flavor. In the same way, our words should preserve what is good and bring life and flavor into conversations. Gospel conversations should not be harsh, stale, or lifeless; they should be seasoned with wisdom, truth, and hope. Proverbs 25:11 says, *A word spoken at the right time is like gold apples in silver settings.* The right word, spoken with grace, can have eternal impact.

Paul adds, *so that you may know how you should answer each person.* Notice the emphasis on *each person.* Evangelism is not one-size-fits-all. Different people need different approaches. Some need comfort; others need challenge. Some are ready for deep Bible study; others are just beginning to ask questions. The wise Christian listens well, asks questions, and responds with sensitivity to the person in front of them.

Think of a doctor prescribing medicine. He doesn't give every patient the same prescription; he listens, diagnoses, and provides what is needed.

In the same way, when we talk with people about Jesus, we listen to their story and then respond with the truth of the gospel in a way that speaks to their need.

Practically, this means learning to speak naturally about Christ in everyday conversations. Instead of forcing the gospel awkwardly, we can let it flow out of who we are. It might mean sharing how prayer helps you through stress, how Scripture gives you direction, or how Christ gave you forgiveness. Short, grace-filled words open the door to deeper discussions. The call is clear: live wisely, but also speak graciously. Our lives draw attention, and our words explain. Together, they form a powerful witness to the hope of Christ.

Practical Application: How to Share Your Faith

Sharing your faith can feel intimidating, but it doesn't have to be. Scripture reminds us that evangelism is not about polished speeches but about living with wisdom, speaking with grace, and being ready to point to the hope we have in Christ. Here are some practical ways to put this into action:

1. **Identify Your Circle**
   Write down two or three people in your life who don't yet know Christ. They may be friends, co-workers, neighbors, or even family members. Begin praying daily for them by name, asking God to open doors and prepare their hearts.
2. **Practice Your Testimony**
   Prepare a simple way to share your story of faith in two or three minutes. Focus on three points: (1) What your life was like without Christ, (2) What Christ has done for you, and (3) The hope you now have in Him. This makes you ready when opportunities arise.
3. **Watch for Open Doors**
   Pay attention to everyday conversations. When someone shares a struggle, express compassion and let them know how Christ helps you in similar situations. Opportunities often come disguised as casual comments.
4. **Speak Naturally, Not Formally**
   You don't need to launch into a sermon. Just weave your faith into

ordinary life. For example: "When I was going through something like that, prayer made such a difference for me." These simple words open the door for deeper conversations.

5. **Follow Up with Scripture**
   When opportunities arise, share a verse that has impacted you. Don't overwhelm; just offer one passage and explain why it matters. God's Word is powerful... often more persuasive than anything we can say.

Challenge

This week, pray for one open door and one moment of courage to walk through it. When God provides that opportunity, don't over-complicate it ... simply share your hope in Christ with grace, humility, and confidence.

Conclusion

Sharing our faith is one of the greatest privileges and responsibilities God has given us. Peter reminds us to be ready to answer the hope within us, and Paul reminds us to live wisely and speak graciously so that our witness is credible and clear. Evangelism is not reserved for experts or preachers; it is the calling of every believer. It is not about winning debates or delivering perfect speeches but about pointing people to Jesus: the source of our hope.

The truth is, God has already placed people in your life who need to hear the gospel. Neighbors, co-workers, friends, or family members are watching how you live and listening to how you speak. Your consistent life, your gracious words, and your readiness to share your story may be the very things God uses to draw them closer to Christ.

The challenge is simple: live wisely, speak graciously, and be ready. This week, ask God to open one door for you to share your faith, and then step into that moment with humility and courage. Remember, you don't need to have every answer; you just need to point to the One who is the answer.

For Discussion

1. Can you recall a time when someone shared their faith with you in a simple but meaningful way? What stood out to you about their approach?

2. Peter says we should "always be ready to give a defense for the hope that is in you." What does readiness look like in practical, everyday terms? How can you prepare yourself to share?

3. How does our daily conduct open or close doors for gospel conversations? Can you think of examples where someone's life validated (or undermined) their words?

4. Why is the tone of our words just as important as the content when we share our faith? How can we season our words with "salt" in conversations about Christ?

5. Of the five applications we discussed (identifying your circle, practicing your testimony, watching for open doors, speaking naturally, sharing Scripture), which one feels most doable for you right now? Which one feels most challenging?

6. Who is one person God has placed in your life that you can begin praying for and seeking opportunities to share Christ with this week?

___

___

___

Part Two

Relational Tools

Ministry is carried out in community. God has designed His people to serve and grow together, using their gifts in harmony with one another. In this section, we will explore the relational tools that enable believers to build strong spiritual connections: serving with our gifts, mentoring and being mentored, bearing one another's burdens, and practicing hospitality. These tools remind us that ministry is not an isolated effort but a shared calling in which we help one another grow in faith, maturity, and love.

Lesson 5

How to Serve Others with Your Gifts

Romans 12:3–8; 1 Corinthians 12:12–17

For by the grace given to me, I tell everyone among you not to think of himself more highly than he should think. Instead, think sensibly, as God has distributed a measure of faith to each one. Now as we have many parts in one body, and all the parts do not have the same function, in the same way we who are many are one body in Christ and individually members of one another. According to the grace given to us, we have different gifts: If prophecy, use it according to the proportion of one's faith; if service, use it in service; if teaching, in teaching; if exhorting, in exhortation; giving, with generosity; leading, with diligence; showing mercy, with cheerfulness,
Romans 12:3–8.

Class Overview: Every Christian has been uniquely equipped by God with gifts to serve others and build up the church. From Romans 12:3–8 and 1 Corinthians 12:12–27, we learn that the body of Christ functions best when every member recognizes their place, values others, and serves in love. These gifts are not about position or prestige—they are about participation. God has arranged each part of the body with purpose, and when every believer uses their gifts with humility and love, the church grows strong, unified, and effective in its mission. This lesson challenges us to identify our God-given gifts and put them to use for the good of others and the glory of Christ.

Class Objectives:

By the end of this class, you should be able to:

1. Understand the source of spiritual gifts
2. Recognize the unity and diversity of the Body
3. Serve in love for the common good
4. Develop practical habits of service

5. Encourage and affirm one another's gifts
6. Live out the challenge of service

Introduction:

It feels like we've had a lot of funerals in our congregation since the pandemic that began the decade. I know that in my preaching, I have conducted more funerals in the last five years than in the first 10. After one of our church members passed a few years ago, I watched something remarkable happen. The family had been through a long and exhausting week, and the church gathered to provide a meal. What struck me wasn't just the food itself, but how everyone contributed in their own way. Some cooked, some set up tables, and some cleaned afterward. None of the work was glamorous, but every part mattered. Together, they served with love, and in that moment, the church looked exactly like what God designed it to be: one body, many members, each using their gift for the good of others.

Moments like that remind me that ministry is not the job of a few; it's the calling of all. God has placed within each believer unique abilities, passions, and opportunities to serve. Romans 12:6 says, *According to the grace given to us, we have different gifts.* Paul reminds us that the church functions like a body; different parts, each with its own role, working together under one head, Christ (1 Corinthians 12:12–27). When one member serves faithfully, everyone benefits; when one member withholds their gift, the whole body feels the loss.

Too often, we underestimate what God has placed within us. We assume that ministry belongs to those who preach, teach, or lead, but Scripture tells a different story. Every Christian is gifted. Every Christian is needed. And every gift, whether public or private, visible or unseen, matters deeply to God.

As we study this lesson, we'll see that serving others through our gifts is both an act of humility and an act of love. God gives the gifts, but He calls us to use them, not to glorify ourselves, but to build up the body and advance His mission.

So, here's the question we'll explore: *How can we discover and use our gifts in ways that strengthen others, honor God, and bring unity to the body of Christ?*

God Gives Gifts to Every Child of His

In Romans 12:3–6a, we find an important reminder about perspective: *for by the grace given to me, I tell everyone among you not to think of himself more highly than he should think. Instead, think sensibly, as God has distributed a measure of faith to each one.* (v. 3). Before Paul ever lists spiritual gifts, he calls for humility. Serving others starts not with pride over what we can do, but gratitude for what God has given.

The phrase "God has distributed" reminds us that spiritual gifts are not earned; they are entrusted. They are given by grace, not merit. None of us can boast, because every ability, opportunity, and resource comes from the same source: God. And that means every Christian has a gift. There are no "ungifted" believers. Every member of the body has something to contribute to the health and growth of the church.

Paul writes in verse 4, *now as we have many parts in one body, and all the parts do not have the same function, in the same way we who are many are one body in Christ and individually members of one another.* This image of the body is brilliant. Just as your hands, eyes, and ears have different functions but all serve one purpose, so too, in the church, the diversity of gifts serves the unity of mission. The variety of gifts reflects the creativity and wisdom of God Himself.

I once worked for a congregation where one of the most faithful servants was a quiet man who kept the baptistry up. He made sure the water was clean and the heater worked. He never stood on the stage, never led a prayer, but his gift made baptism as comfortable as possible. Another sister spent hours each week writing notes to new Christians. Neither sought attention, but both were indispensable. Their gifts, though different, flowed from the same Spirit and served the same purpose: to build up the body of Christ.

That's what Paul means when he says in verse 6, *that according to the grace given to us, we have different gifts.* God designed the church to function best when everyone recognizes and uses what He's given them. The danger arises when we start comparing, wishing we had someone else's gift, or assuming our contribution doesn't matter. But comparison destroys ministry. God doesn't expect you to serve with someone else's gift; He calls you to be faithful with your own.

So, what does this mean for us? First, it means **humility**, remembering that our gifts are grace, not status. Second, it means **responsibility**, realizing that unused gifts are wasted opportunities. And third, it means **joy**, because serving in the way God designed you brings deep satisfaction and purpose. When each member uses their gift, the body becomes a living testimony of God's wisdom and love.

Different Gifts, One Body

In 1 Corinthians 12:12–20, Paul expands on the metaphor of the body, writing, *for just as the body is one and has many parts, and all the parts of that body, though many, are one body, so also is Christ* (v. 12). It's a simple image, but it carries a simple truth. The church is not an organization or a social club; it is a living organism. Each member of the family is a vital part of that body, joined to Christ the Head, and connected in purpose and function.

In verse 13, Paul explains the unity behind this diversity: *for we were all baptized by one Spirit into one body, whether Jews or Greeks, whether slaves or free, and we were all given one Spirit to drink.* No matter our background, personality, or ability, we were all brought into the same family through the same Spirit. That's what makes the church beautiful. God takes people who have nothing in common by the world's standards and weaves them together in perfect unity through His Spirit.

Paul then uses a touch of humor to make his point. He says, *if the foot should say, 'Because I'm not a hand, I don't belong to the body,' it is not for that reason any less a part of the body. And if the ear should say, 'Because I'm not an eye, I don't belong to the body,' it is not for that reason any less a part of the body* (vv. 15–16). You can almost picture the conversation, a talking foot jealous of a hand, an ear feeling overlooked compared to the eye. But Paul's point is clear: every part is essential.

We live in a culture that celebrates some roles while overlooking others. The same danger can creep into the church, where preachers, teachers, or leaders are viewed as more "important" than those who quietly serve behind the scenes. But in God's design, there are no unimportant parts. The preacher may proclaim the gospel, but someone else greets visitors, cleans the building, manages technology, prepares communion, or comforts the grieving. Each one contributes to Christ's mission.

Paul concludes in verse 18, *but as it is, God has arranged each one of the parts in the body just as He wanted.* That's the key, *God* arranged it. You are not in the body by accident. Your gifts, your story, your abilities, they are intentional. God placed you where you are for a reason. And verse 19 drives it home: *if they were all the same part, where would the body be?* In other words, uniformity is not the goal, unity is.

Practically, this means we should celebrate our differences rather than compete with them. The church doesn't need everyone to be the same; it needs everyone to serve. When one member suffers, the whole body hurts; when one member thrives, the whole body rejoices (v. 26). That's the beauty of the body of Christ: unity in diversity, held together by the Spirit, working together for God's glory.

Serving in Love for the Common Good

After describing the diversity of gifts within the body, Paul moves to how those gifts should be used. In Romans 12:6–8 he writes, *according to the grace given to us, we have different gifts: if prophecy, use it according to the proportion of one's faith; if service, use it in service; if teaching, in teaching; if exhorting, in exhortation; giving, with generosity; leading, with diligence; showing mercy, with cheerfulness.*

Notice the emphasis: whatever your gift is, *use it.* Paul doesn't just list abilities; he gives instructions for how to use them: with faith, with generosity, with diligence, with cheerfulness. Spiritual gifts are not decorations to admire; they are tools to employ. God did not give us gifts to store on a shelf but to put into motion for the good of others.

The same theme appears in 1 Corinthians 12:25–27, where Paul says the purpose of our different roles is *that there would be no division in the body, but that the members would have the same concern for each other.* The goal of our gifts is not competition but compassion. When we serve with love, the body is strengthened and unity deepens.

This is why spiritual gifts cannot be divorced from love. Right after describing the gifts in 1 Corinthians 12, Paul flows straight into 1 Corinthians 13: the great love chapter. The connection is deliberate. Without love, even the most impressive gifts mean nothing. You can teach with brilliance, serve with energy, or give with sacrifice, but if love is absent, it profits nothing (1 Corinthians 13:1–3). Love is the motivation, the safeguard, and the measure of all ministry.

I once knew a man whose gift was encouragement. He wasn't flashy or loud, but every week he found someone to lift up: a teenager, a widow, a tired parent. He'd shake hands and quietly remind people that they mattered. He was one of several who helped shift the congregation's tone. You could feel the warmth of love growing in the body. His gift wasn't about recognition; it was about building others up for the common good. Even after I moved to another congregation, he remained a constant source of encouragement to me. Every year, he would drive from the next state over to be part of our annual men's retreat. When he passed away suddenly several years back, Christians from all over the Midwest were impacted.

That's how God intends His church to work. When each person uses their gift, not for attention, but for love, the church flourishes. The teacher builds faith through knowledge. The servant meets needs with compassion. The encourager restores hope through words. The giver supplies resources with joy. The leader guides with diligence. Each role, motivated by love, blesses the whole body.

So, what does this mean for us? It means we should:

- **Use our gifts:** Don't wait for perfect conditions, start serving where you are.
- **Serve with the right heart:** Love must be the reason behind what we do.
- **Honor others' gifts:** Celebrate what they bring rather than comparing or competing.

- **Keep the mission in focus:** Our gifts are for the *common good,* to glorify Christ and build His church.

When we serve in love, the church becomes a living picture of Christ Himself, diverse, unified, and overflowing with grace. Every act of service, no matter how small, becomes a declaration of love for God and for His people.

Practical Application: How to Serve Others with Your Gifts

Discovering and using your spiritual gifts isn't a mysterious process: it's a matter of faith, humility, and love. God has already given you what you need to serve. The key is to recognize it, develop it, and use it for the good of others. Here are some practical ways to put this lesson into action:

1. **Discover Your Gifts Through Service**
   Spiritual gifts are best discovered by doing, not by waiting. Get involved in something: teaching, serving, visiting, mentoring, giving. As you step into opportunities, you'll begin to recognize what energizes you and blesses others. Gifts reveal themselves in motion, not in theory.
2. **Ask Others What They See in You**
   Sometimes others can see your gifts more clearly than you can. Ask a trusted Christian friend or leader: "Where do you see me being most effective in serving others?" Their insight can help you identify how God has uniquely shaped you.
3. **Start Small, But Start**
   You don't have to overhaul your life or take on a significant ministry role. Begin with one consistent act of service, a class to help with, a person to visit, a note to send, a meal to prepare. God often turns small acts of faithfulness into greater opportunities.
4. **Use Your Gifts with the Right Attitude**
   Paul says to use your gift *with diligence, with generosity, and with cheerfulness.* The heart matters as much as the action. Serve not for recognition, but for love. Remember that unseen acts of service are often the ones most honored by God.

5. **Celebrate the Gifts of Others**
   Instead of comparing or competing, thank God for the variety of gifts in the body. Express appreciation to those who serve differently from you, the teacher, the encourager, the organizer, the giver. A healthy church celebrates the diversity of its members' ministries.

Challenge

This week, prayerfully identify one area of ministry where you can actively use your gifts to serve others. Commit to one concrete act of service that strengthens the body of Christ, whether that means helping, teaching, visiting, or simply encouraging. Then take a moment to thank someone else for the way they're using *their* gift.

Conclusion

The beauty of the church is found in its diversity: many members, many gifts, yet one purpose. God designed His body to thrive not when a few do much, but when everyone does their part. As Paul writes, *"From Him the whole body, fitted and knit together by every supporting ligament, promotes the growth of the body for building itself up in love by the proper working of each individual part"* (Ephesians 4:16). The church grows strongest when every member serves.

We've seen that our gifts are given by grace, meant for the good of others, and powered by love. They are not trophies to display or talents to compare, but tools to use. Some gifts are public, others quiet and unseen, but all are necessary. The person who teaches from the pulpit and the one who comforts in the hallway are equally vital to the body of Christ.

The question for each of us is simple: *What am I doing with what God has given me?* Every gift matters, and when we withhold ours, the body suffers. But when we serve with humility and love, something extraordinary happens: Christ's character is displayed through His people. The church becomes a living, breathing picture of grace in action.

So, the challenge this week is clear: thank God for the gifts He's given you, commit to using them for His glory, and look for someone else's gift to affirm. When each of us serves with love, the body is strengthened, the mission advances, and God is glorified.

For Discussion

1. Can you recall a time when someone's act of service, even a small one, made a major impact on your life or faith? What did it show you about how the body of Christ works together?

   ____

   ____

   ____

2. Why does Paul begin his teaching on spiritual gifts with a call to humility? How does humility change the way we view our own gifts and the gifts of others?

   ____

   ____

   ____

3. Paul compares the church to a body with many parts. What are some practical ways we can value "less visible" members and roles in the church?

   ____

   ____

   ____

4. What happens when people serve without love? How does love keep our service from becoming self-centered or competitive?

   ____

   ____

   ____

5. Of the five application points (discover your gifts, ask others, start small, serve with the right attitude, celebrate others' gifts), which

one do you need to act on most? What's one small way you can begin this week?

___

___

___

6. How would your local congregation change if every member used their God-given gifts faithfully? What part can you play in helping that vision become reality?

___

___

___

Lesson 6

How to Mentor and Be Mentored

2 Timothy 2:1–2; Acts 18:24–28

You, therefore, my son, be strong in the grace that is in Christ Jesus. What you have heard from me in the presence of many witnesses, commit to faithful men who will be able to teach others also, 2 Timothy 2:1–2.

Class Overview: Spiritual growth is never meant to happen in isolation; it flourishes in relationships. From Paul's words to Timothy (2 Timothy 2:1–2) to the quiet example of Aquila and Priscilla guiding Apollos (Acts 18:24–28), Scripture shows that mentoring is God's method for multiplying faith. Every Christian should be both a learner and a teacher, strengthened by others while helping others grow. Mentoring is not about hierarchy but about humility and investment; it's the passing of truth, wisdom, and encouragement from one generation to the next. This lesson challenges us to build intentional relationships that strengthen disciples, reproduce ministry, and carry the gospel forward.

Class Objectives:

By the end of this class, you should be able to:

1. Explain Paul's model of spiritual multiplication in 2 Timothy 2:1–2 and identify how it applies in the local church today.
2. Describe how Aquila and Priscilla's relationship with Apollos (Acts 18:24–26) demonstrates wisdom, humility, and grace in guiding others.
3. Understand that every Christian should both seek guidance from mentors and invest in others to continue the chain of discipleship.
4. Commit to intentional, consistent relationships that include prayer, Scripture study, accountability, and encouragement.
5. Learn to offer correction and guidance in a spirit of gentleness and love, following the example of Aquila and Priscilla.
6. Identify one person to learn from and one person to mentor, taking an intentional step this week to begin those relationships.

Introduction:

When I first started preaching at age 21, I was young, nervous, and inexperienced. I remember standing before the congregation one Sunday evening, trying to deliver a lesson on the book of Hosea that I had prepared for days. It didn't go well. My voice shook, my thoughts were scattered, and the lesson lasted about ten minutes. I felt utterly defeated. Later, one of the deacons in the congregation was standing in the back near the entryway. I can still see him walking toward me with his familiar smile, putting his arm around my shoulder, and saying, "You did well. Keep going. You're gonna be great."

That man, who recently passed away after a brief battle with a rare cancer, became a mentor and my best friend. He didn't just critique me; he invested in me. He never made me feel small; he helped me grow. To this day, I thank God for that relationship because it shaped not only my preaching but also my heart for ministry.

We all need people like that in our lives, people who help us grow in faith, character, and service. And just as importantly, others need *us* to be that person for them. Mentoring is the heartbeat of spiritual growth. It's how faith is passed from one generation to the next, not just through sermons or classes, but through relationships of trust, love, and accountability.

Paul understood this when he wrote to Timothy, *you, therefore, my son, be strong in the grace that is in Christ Jesus. What you have heard from me in the presence of many witnesses, commit to faithful men who will be able to teach others also* (2 Timothy 2:1–2). In that one verse, we see four generations of faith: Paul, Timothy, faithful men, and those they would teach. This is God's blueprint for spiritual multiplication. The faith we've received is not meant to stop with us; it's intended to continue through us.

We see this same pattern in Acts 18, where Aquila and Priscilla take Apollos aside and mentor him privately. They help him understand "the way of God more accurately," and as a result, Apollos becomes a powerful teacher of the gospel. Mentoring fosters maturity; it transforms learners into leaders.

So today, as we explore this lesson, we'll ask two key questions: *Who is pouring into you?* and *Who are you pouring into?* Every Christian should be both a student and a teacher—learning from others while helping others grow. That's how the church stays strong, how the mission moves forward, and how God's grace continues from one generation to the next.

The Pattern of Spiritual Multiplication

Paul's words to Timothy in 2 Timothy 2:1–2 capture one of the clearest pictures of mentorship in all of Scripture: *you, therefore, my son, be strong in the grace that is in Christ Jesus. What you have heard from me in the presence of many witnesses, commit to faithful men who will be able to teach others also.* These verses describe a chain of discipleship that extends across generations: Paul to Timothy, Timothy to faithful men, and those men to others. This is not just addition; it's multiplication. Paul's goal was not merely to teach Timothy; it was to equip Timothy to teach others who would then teach others again.

Notice how this begins: *be strong in the grace that is in Christ Jesus.* Mentoring starts with strength rooted in grace, not ego. Paul isn't telling Timothy to be strong in personality, intellect, or experience, but in grace: the divine strength that flows from a relationship with Christ. True mentoring is never about creating followers of us; it's about developing followers of Jesus.

Paul's instruction, *what you have heard from me... commit to faithful men,* shows that mentoring is intentional. The word *commit* (or *entrust*) carries the idea of depositing something valuable for safekeeping. The gospel is a treasure, and we are stewards of that treasure. Mentorship is how that treasure is carefully, personally, and purposefully passed along.

Imagine a relay race. The runners' success depends not only on speed but on how well they pass the baton. Drop the baton, and the race is lost. Paul is urging Timothy: *Don't drop the baton.* What you've received, pass on faithfully to others who can continue the race after you. Mentoring is the handoff that keeps the mission moving forward.

The verse also reminds us that not everyone is ready for that responsibility. Paul tells Timothy to commit truth to "faithful men," those who are reliable, teachable, and committed to growth. Mentorship isn't about popularity or talent; it's about character and faithfulness. It's better to invest deeply in a few faithful people than to spread shallow influence over many.

Practically, this means we should all think in terms of spiritual multiplication. Who poured into you, and who are you pouring into? Who will carry your influence forward after you? For elders, preachers, teachers, parents, and mature Christians, the call is the same: don't let the work stop with you. Train someone to carry it further. For younger believers, the call is to seek guidance and learn from those who have walked faithfully ahead of you.

This is how the gospel has spread for two thousand years: one relationship at a time, from Paul to Timothy, from Timothy to others, and from those others to us. Mentorship isn't a program; it's God's method for multiplying faith.

The Power of Mentoring Relationships

In Acts 18:24–26, we're introduced to a man named Apollos, a gifted, eloquent, and passionate teacher from Alexandria. Luke describes him as *competent in the Scriptures… instructed in the way of the Lord… and speaking and teaching accurately about Jesus, although he only knew John's baptism* (vv. 24–25). Apollos had zeal and ability, but his knowledge was incomplete. Then something beautiful happened: *after Priscilla and Aquila heard him, they took him aside and explained the way of God to him more accurately* (v. 26).

This moment illustrates the quiet, transformative power of mentoring. Aquila and Priscilla didn't embarrass Apollos or argue publicly. They didn't correct him harshly or undermine his confidence. Instead, they *took him aside*, privately, gently, and personally, and helped him grow. They combined truth with love, instruction with grace. That's the heart of mentoring.

Mentoring always involves a relationship. It's not about lectures or criticism from a distance; it's about walking alongside someone, speaking truth into their life, and helping them see what they can't yet see. Aquila and Priscilla modeled humility as well; they were tentmakers, not apostles or scholars. But their love for God and understanding of His Word made them powerful mentors.

We often underestimate the power of quiet, personal investment. It doesn't need to be dramatic or formal. It could be an older Christian regularly meeting with a younger Christian for Bible study and prayer. It might be a godly couple mentoring a young couple on marriage and family. It could be an experienced teacher guiding someone new on how to study and lead effectively. The strongest churches are those where these kinds of relationships happen naturally, across generations, genders, and experiences.

For those who are mature in the faith, this passage challenges us to recognize *potential.* Aquila and Priscilla could have ignored Apollos or assumed someone else would correct him. Instead, they saw what he *could become* with guidance. For those who are younger in faith, this passage calls us to accept *correction.* Apollos didn't resist or take offense; he listened and learned, and as we'll see next, his growth multiplied his impact.

Mentoring relationships like this strengthen the whole body. When we take time to teach, encourage, and guide others, the truth of God's Word is preserved, and His people are equipped for greater service.

The Partnership of Learning and Teaching

After Aquila and Priscilla mentored Apollos, something powerful happened. Luke writes, *when he wanted to cross over to Achaia, the brothers and sisters wrote to the disciples to welcome him. After he arrived, he was a great help to those who by grace had believed. For he vigorously refuted the Jews in public, demonstrating through the Scriptures that Jesus is the Messiah* (Acts 18:27–28).

This is the fruit of mentoring. The man who once had incomplete knowledge of the gospel became a confident and effective defender of the faith. Notice that the story didn't end with correction; it continued with *multiplication.* Aquila and Priscilla poured into Apollos; he then went out and poured into others. That's the divine pattern: those who are taught become teachers; those who are strengthened become strengtheners.

This partnership between learning and teaching is what keeps the church vibrant and healthy. The Christian life is never static. We are constantly learning from others and teaching others. There's never a point where we arrive. Even Paul, late in his ministry, told the Philippians, *not that I have already reached the goal or am already perfect, but I make every effort to take hold of it because I also have been taken hold of by Christ Jesus* (Philippians 3:12). The humble heart is always teachable. The grateful heart is always eager to teach.

Mentoring is not a one-way street; it's a cycle of growth. Apollos's example shows us that we can both receive and give, learning from those ahead of us and helping those behind us. Healthy churches are filled with this rhythm: older women teaching younger women (Titus 2:3–5), experienced Christians guiding new converts, parents training children in faith, and younger members bringing fresh energy and encouragement to their mentors. Each generation strengthens the next.

Reflecting on my own experience as a young preacher, there was a group of elders and an experienced preacher I worked with in Indiana who believed in me before I believed in myself. Those two elders welcomed me into their homes, stopped by my office for encouragement, took me to gospel meetings, and studied with me. The preacher worked with me tirelessly day after day. Both elders have since passed away, and the preacher is now aging, but they truly transformed my life. Whenever I have the opportunity, I mentor others in the same way: passing on the encouragement I once received. That's precisely what God intends.

We all need both sides of this partnership. We need mentors who challenge and shape us, and we need to invest in others intentionally. This could mean helping a new Christian develop in prayer or Bible study. It might involve guiding a younger couple through marriage challenges. It could also mean training a young teacher, deacon, or future elder. When we invest in others, we expand our ministry.

Apollos's story reminds us that when mentoring relationships thrive, the gospel advances. The church gains strength, truth spreads, and faith is reproduced. Each of us is called to take what we've received and pass it on: faithfully, humbly, and with love.

Practical Application: How to Mentor and Be Mentored

Mentoring isn't a formal program or title; it's a way of life centered on discipleship. It occurs when we intentionally seek to help a brother or sister grow in faith. Every Christian can take part in this, regardless of age, experience, or church role. Here are some practical ways to get started:

1. **Seek Out a Mentor**
   Identify someone whose faith, wisdom, or example inspires you. Ask them to meet occasionally for conversation, prayer, or Bible study. Don't wait for them to approach you; take initiative. A simple, "I'd love to learn from you. Could we meet once a month?" can begin a life-changing relationship.
2. **Be a Mentor to Someone Else**
   Look for someone younger in faith or life experience, a new Christian, a young couple, a teen, or even a peer. Ask how you can help them grow. Mentoring doesn't mean you have all the answers; it means you're willing to walk beside someone, listen, and point them toward Christ.
3. **Make Mentoring Intentional**
   Set aside time. Meet regularly, even if it's just once a month. Study a book of the Bible together, share prayer requests, and talk about challenges. Don't let busyness crowd it out. Mentorship thrives on consistency.
4. **Keep It Personal and Relational**
   Notice how Aquila and Priscilla took Apollos *aside.* Mentoring works best in safe, honest, and humble spaces. Be approachable. Share your own struggles and lessons learned. Authenticity builds trust.
5. **Multiply the Pattern**
   Encourage those you mentor to do the same for others. This is the heartbeat of 2 Timothy 2:2, passing faith forward. When you help one person grow, you strengthen generations to come.
6. **Let Grace Lead**
   Paul told Timothy, *"Be strong in the grace that is in Christ Jesus."*

Remember, mentoring is not about control or correction alone; it's about grace. Extend patience, forgiveness, and encouragement as others grow, just as others once did for you.

Challenge

This week, identify one person you can learn from and one person you can invest in. Reach out to both. Begin a conversation, schedule a meeting, or send a note of encouragement. Then, pray that God will use these relationships to strengthen faith, deepen love, and multiply the gospel for years to come.

Conclusion

The story of Paul and Timothy, along with Aquila, Priscilla, and Apollos, reminds us that faith was never meant to be lived alone. God designed spiritual growth to happen through relationships. We become stronger when someone invests in us, and we grow deeper when we invest in others. Mentoring is the link that connects one generation of faith to the next.

We've seen that spiritual multiplication starts with grace, as Paul told Timothy: *Be strong in the grace that is in Christ Jesus.* It progresses through intentional relationships, such as those of Aquila and Priscilla, who patiently guided Apollos toward a deeper understanding of the truth. And it produces fruit when those who are taught begin teaching others, creating a continuous chain of discipleship that advances the gospel.

Every Christian has a role in that chain. Some of us need to be humble enough to seek guidance and correction, while others need to be courageous enough to step forward and mentor those coming behind. When the church embraces both roles, learning and teaching, receiving and giving, the result is a living picture of Christ's body working together in grace and truth.

Don't let your faith end with you. Take what you've learned and pass it on. Find a mentor who will strengthen you and a disciple who will challenge you. Build intentional relationships that deepen faith, expand ministry, and honor God. When we do this, we keep the chain of grace alive, from one believer to another, from one generation to the next, until the Lord returns.

For Discussion

1. Who has been a mentor or spiritual influence in your life? What specific qualities or actions made their influence meaningful?

   ____
   ____
   ____

2. Paul instructed Timothy to pass on what he had learned to others who would teach others also. What does this passage reveal about how God intends faith to spread? How can we live out that pattern today?

   ____
   ____
   ____

3. How did Aquila and Priscilla model wise and loving mentorship with Apollos? What lessons can we learn from their example about how to approach others who need guidance or correction?

   ____
   ____
   ____

4. Apollos grew under mentorship, then used his growth to strengthen others. How have you seen this "learn and teach" cycle at work in your own life or in your congregation?

   ____
   ____
   ____

5. What are some simple ways to start a mentoring relationship, whether you're a mentor or a learner? What obstacles sometimes prevent us from forming those connections, and how can we overcome them?

___

___

___

6. Who is one person you could learn from, and one person you could invest in this month? What first step could you take this week to begin those relationships?

___

___

___

Lesson 7

How to Bear Burdens

Galatians 6:1–3

Brothers and sisters, if someone is overtaken in any wrongdoing, you who are spiritual, restore such a person with a gentle spirit, watching out for yourselves so that you also won't be tempted. Carry one another's burdens; in this way you will fulfill the law of Christ. For if anyone considers himself to be something when he is nothing, he deceives himself, Galatians 6:1–3.

Class Overview: The Christian life was never meant to be lived alone. God designed the church as a community of compassion where believers share one another's struggles. From Galatians 6:1–2 and Romans 15:1–2, we learn that bearing burdens is not just an act of kindness; it is how we fulfill the law of Christ, the law of love. Mature Christians don't criticize the fallen; they restore them gently. The strong don't distance themselves from the weak; they carry them. When we lift together, we grow together. This lesson calls believers to embody the heart of Jesus by walking alongside others in their suffering, restoring the broken, and serving the weary, turning love into action and grace into strength.

Class Objectives:

By the end of this class, you should be able to:

1. Explain the meaning of Galatians 6:1–2 and how bearing burdens fulfills the "law of Christ."
2. Describe the qualities needed to restore others, humility, gentleness, and self-awareness, and why they are essential in burden-bearing.
3. Understand from Romans 15:1–2 that strength is given for service, not self-pleasure, and that helping the weak strengthens the entire body.
4. Identify specific ways to support those struggling, through prayer, presence, listening, and tangible help.
5. Commit to building relationships marked by empathy and patience, where believers feel safe to share their burdens.

6. Choose one person this week to encourage or assist, intentionally lightening their load as an expression of Christlike love.

Introduction:

I REMEMBER A SEASON IN MY LIFE when things felt especially heavy. It wasn't one big crisis, just a collection of smaller weights…long days, unexpected setbacks, and the quiet exhaustion that builds up over time. One afternoon, after a tough week, a sister from church sent me the nicest text message. She had read one of my lessons on my blog and told me how encouraged she was and how glad she was that I was her preacher. After reading, the circumstances hadn't changed, but something in me had. The load felt lighter because someone else had chosen to encourage me.

That's what Paul means when he says: *carry one another's burdens; in this way you will fulfill the law of Christ* (Galatians 6:2). To bear another's burden is to step into their struggle, not to fix it, but to share it. It's the practical expression of love that reflects the heart of Jesus, who bore our greatest burden, the weight of sin, upon Himself (Isaiah 53:4–6).

In the church, burden-bearing is one of the clearest marks of maturity and compassion. It's easy to care from a distance, to say, "I'll pray for you," without truly entering into someone's pain. But love moves closer. Love listens, helps, and stands beside those who are weary. Paul says in Romans 15:1–2, *we who are strong have an obligation to bear the weaknesses of those without strength, and not to please ourselves.* In other words, the stronger believer doesn't use strength for self, but to lift up the weak.

Ministry isn't just about teaching, praying, or serving; it's about carrying. And when we carry burdens together, we fulfill the law of Christ, the law of love. This lesson will show us that bearing burdens is not optional; it is the natural outcome of grace. We'll learn that it takes humility, maturity, and courage to step into another person's pain, but when we do, we look most like Jesus.

So, let's ask ourselves as we begin: *Whose burden is God calling me to help carry this week?*

Bearing Burdens Reflects the Heart of Christ

In Galatians 6:1–2, Paul writes, *carry one another's burdens; in this way you will fulfill the law of Christ.* The phrase "law of Christ" points back to Jesus' command in John 13:34: *I give you a new command: Love one another. Just as I have loved you, you are also to love one another.* In other words, to bear another's burden is to love as Jesus loved. It is to step into someone else's pain with the same compassion Christ showed when He stepped into ours.

To "carry" here means to shoulder or lift something heavy that another person cannot carry alone. The word for "burden" refers to a crushing weight, something that presses down so hard it becomes unbearable. We all have moments when life feels like that: grief that won't lift, sin that won't loosen its grip, worry that won't fade. And when those moments come, God calls His people to step in and carry the load together.

This command is more than an act of kindness; it is an act of Christlikeness. Jesus bore our burdens, not metaphorically, but literally. Isaiah 53:4 says, *He Himself bore our sicknesses, and He carried our pains.* On the cross, He took the full weight of our sin and shame. So, when we carry each other's burdens, we are imitating the very heart of Jesus. We become His hands, His feet, and His heart in a hurting world.

Bearing burdens doesn't always mean solving problems. Sometimes it means sitting quietly beside someone who is hurting. Sometimes it means praying for them when they can't find the words. Sometimes it means meeting a physical need: a meal, a ride, a visit, or financial help. Whatever form it takes, it always means love in action.

In Galatians 6:2, Paul says that this is how we "fulfill the law of Christ." We fulfill the core of His command when we love not just in theory, but in practice; when we see a need and move toward it, not away from it. The world is full of people who walk by on the other side of the road; Christ calls His followers to be the ones who stop, lift, and carry.

So, when we bear burdens, we are doing far more than helping with a problem: we are displaying the gospel. We are showing the world what grace looks like in flesh and blood.

Bearing Burdens Requires Spiritual Maturity

Paul starts Galatians 6 with an important qualifier: *brothers and sisters, if someone is caught in any wrongdoing, you who are spiritual should restore such a person gently, watching out for yourselves so that you also won't be tempted.* Before we can help carry someone else's burden, we must first be spiritually grounded ourselves. Burden-bearing is not a task for the proud or impatient; it's a ministry for the humble and mature.

The phrase "overtaken in any wrongdoing" illustrates someone caught or trapped by sin, not someone intentionally rebelling against God, but someone who has stumbled and can't seem to recover. The word "restore" means to put something back in its place, like resetting a broken bone or repairing a torn net. The goal isn't punishment or public shame; it's healing and rebuilding. That requires spiritual sensitivity, patience, and love.

Paul says, *you who are spiritual,* meaning those walking by the Spirit, not those who think highly of themselves. The spiritually mature person knows their own weakness. They don't look down on the fallen; they remember how often they've needed grace themselves. That's why Paul immediately adds, *"watching out for yourselves so that you also won't be tempted."* If we approach someone else's sin or struggle with arrogance, we risk falling into pride or even into the same sin.

Imagine a firefighter running into a burning building to rescue someone trapped inside. If he rushes in carelessly, without the proper gear, he risks being overcome by the smoke himself. But if he's prepared, equipped, trained, and cautious, he can pull someone else to safety without being consumed. The same is true in ministry. We can't help others out of their fire if we're still playing too close to the flames.

Gently restoring others is a sign of true maturity. It involves listening more than lecturing, speaking truth with compassion, and offering grace without ignoring sin. Jesus demonstrated this perfectly in John 8 when the woman caught in adultery was brought before Him. He neither condoned her sin nor condemned her soul. He said, *neither do I condemn you. Go, and from now on do not sin anymore.* Grace restored her; truth redirected her.

In practice, this means that burden-bearing requires both tenderness and strength. It's not enabling sin; it's helping a person find their footing again. It's not gossiping about someone's failure; it's standing beside them in love and prayer until they're restored. And it takes spiritual maturity to do that without becoming self-righteous or weary.

Paul's words remind us that maturity isn't measured by how much Bible we know, but by how well we love those who are struggling. Mature Christians don't step over the fallen; they kneel beside them. They lift the broken, help them walk again, and point them back to the grace of Christ, remembering that one day, they may need someone to do the same for them.

Bearing Burdens Strengthens the Church

In Romans 15:1–2, Paul writes, *now we who are strong have an obligation to bear the weaknesses of those without strength, and not to please ourselves. Each one of us is to please his neighbor for his good, to build him up.* In these words, Paul shifts our perspective from the individual to the community. Bearing burdens is not just about compassion; it's about commitment, a commitment to the strength, health, and unity of the church.

The phrase "we who are strong" refers to those who are spiritually mature and stable in faith. But notice what Paul says, strength is not a privilege; it's a responsibility. The strong are obligated to use their strength to help those who are weak. In other words, spiritual maturity isn't measured by how much we know, but by how much we care. The test of strength is not in standing tall but in bending low to lift others.

Paul adds, *not to please ourselves.* That strikes at the root of selfishness. The world says, "Look out for yourself." Christ says, "Look out for one another." True ministry is others-centered. We serve not because it's convenient or comfortable, but because it reflects the heart of the Savior. Jesus Himself "did not please Himself" (Romans 15:3); instead, He bore our weaknesses, reproach, and pain to bring us to God.

Think of a mountain climber roped to his teammates as they ascend together. When one slips, the others bear his weight until he regains his footing. The goal isn't just to reach the summit individually, but to make sure *everyone* reaches it safely. That's how the church works. When one member stumbles, the others hold on and pull together. When one member rejoices, all rejoice. When one suffers, all suffer. That's the unity Paul describes in 1 Corinthians 12:26: a body so connected that the pain of one becomes the concern of all.

Bearing burdens in this way strengthens the church because it builds trust and love. When we see brothers and sisters willing to carry our load, our faith deepens, not only in them, but in God who works through them. A burden-bearing church becomes a refuge for the weary and a testimony to the world. It's a family where no one must pretend to be perfect, because everyone knows grace is real.

In practice, we should look for opportunities to help carry others' loads. Someone may be carrying the burden of grief, another the burden of guilt, another the burden of financial strain, or another the weight of loneliness. The question is not *if* those burdens exist, but *whether we will notice and help bear them.*

When we choose to carry one another's burdens, we strengthen the entire body. We build up faith. We restore unity. And we show the watching world that the love of Christ is alive in His people. The church that stands together stands strong.

Practical Application: How to Bear Burdens

Bearing one another's burdens is not an abstract command; it's something every Christian can practice daily. It begins with open eyes, compassionate hearts, and willing hands. Here are several ways to put this lesson into action:

1. **Be Present in Someone's Pain**
   Often, the greatest gift we can give is simply *being there.* When someone is hurting, don't assume they need advice first; they need presence. A visit, a text, or a prayer can remind them they're not alone. Jesus' presence with the suffering is what comforted people most; our presence can do the same.
2. **Listen Without Judgment**
   When a brother or sister confides a struggle, resist the urge to fix everything or correct immediately. Listen first. Sometimes people just need space to be honest about their burdens. Listening communicates love and creates the safety needed for restoration.
3. **Pray Specifically and Faithfully**
   When someone shares a burden, write it down. Pray by name. Follow up later and ask, "How are you doing?" Prayer is not the least we can do, it's often the most powerful. It invites God into the situation and strengthens both the sufferer and the one interceding.
4. **Offer Tangible Help**
   Burden-bearing often takes practical form: a meal for a grieving family, transportation to appointments, a financial gift in a hard time, childcare for exhausted parents, or just a helping hand. James 2:15–17 reminds us that love without action is empty, real compassion moves.
5. **Restore the Fallen Gently**
   If a brother or sister is struggling spiritually, approach with humility and gentleness (Galatians 6:1). Restoration is an act of grace, not superiority. Remember: our goal is not to expose but to heal, not to shame but to strengthen.
6. **Share Your Own Burdens**
   Burden-bearing works both ways. Many Christians carry their struggles alone because they're afraid to appear weak. Sharing

honestly invites others to carry with you, and it builds authentic fellowship within the church.

Challenge

This week, look for one person who is weighed down by grief, sin, stress, or loneliness, and decide how you can help carry their load. Whether it's through prayer, presence, or practical help, be intentional about fulfilling the law of Christ through love.

Conclusion

When Paul calls us to "carry one another's burdens," he's describing far more than a single act of kindness; he's describing a way of life that mirrors the heart of Christ. Jesus didn't stay distant from our pain; He entered it. He bore our griefs, carried our sorrows, and took upon Himself the crushing weight of our sin. Every time we choose to bear another person's burden, we reflect His love to the world.

We've seen that burden-bearing requires humility, maturity, and compassion. It means walking beside the fallen with gentleness, lifting the weary with patience, and serving the weak with strength. It means refusing to stand at a distance when others struggle, because in Christ's body, no one walks alone.

The church is never more beautiful than when it bears burdens together. When we listen without judgment, restore without pride, and serve without self-interest, the world sees what the gospel looks like in real life. Burden-bearing turns abstract love into visible grace.

Look around this week and ask God to show you one person carrying a heavy load. Step into their story. Pray with them. Help them. Listen. Serve. You might not be able to remove the burden entirely, but you can make sure they don't carry it alone. When we do that, when we lift together, we fulfill the law of Christ, strengthen the family of God, and remind one another that grace always meets us in the weight of our weakness.

For Discussion

1. Can you think of a time when someone helped carry your burden, through prayer, encouragement, or simple presence? How did their support strengthen your faith?

 ____

2. Paul says that when we carry one another's burdens, we "fulfill the law of Christ." What does this teach us about the connection between love and action in the Christian life?

3. Why does Paul emphasize that those who are "spiritual" should restore the fallen "with a gentle spirit"? What does this reveal about the attitude required to bear others' burdens well?

4. According to Paul, the strong have an *obligation* to bear the weaknesses of others. How does this challenge our natural tendency to focus on ourselves or our own comfort?

5. What are some real, tangible ways our congregation could become more intentional about burden-bearing? What kinds of needs often go unnoticed or unspoken among us?

6. Who is one person God may be calling you to help this week? How could you lighten their load, spiritually, emotionally, or physically, in a way that fulfills the law of Christ?

Lesson 8

How to Encourage Leaders

Hebrews 13:7, 17; 1 Thessalonians 5:12–13

Remember your leaders who have spoken God's word to you. As you carefully observe the outcome of their lives, imitate their faith, Hebrews 13:7.

Obey your leaders and submit to them, since they keep watch over your souls as those who will give an account, so that they can do this with joy and not with grief, for that would be unprofitable for you, Hebrews 13:17.

Class Overview: Church leaders carry a sacred and often heavy responsibility as they watch over the souls of God's people. Hebrews 13 and 1 Thessalonians 5 remind us that these men and women labor not for recognition, but out of love for the Lord and His church. The strength and joy of leadership depend significantly on the congregation's encouragement and cooperation. When Christians remember their leaders' example, support them with humility, and esteem them in love, the whole body thrives in unity and peace. This lesson reminds us that encouragement is not flattery; it is faithfulness. As we pray for, honor, and assist our leaders, we not only bless them but also honor Christ, the Chief Shepherd of the church.

Class Objectives:

By the end of this class, you should be able to:

1. Explain why Scripture calls believers to remember, respect, and follow those who lead in the Lord (Heb. 13:7, 17; 1 Thess. 5:12–13).
2. Describe what it means for leaders to "keep watch over your souls" and how this should shape our attitude toward them.
3. Identify practical ways to encourage leaders through prayer, gratitude, cooperation, and acts of kindness.
4. Commit to guarding unity by refusing gossip, criticism, or disrespect that undermines leadership and harms the church's witness.
5. Cultivate a spirit of appreciation that values leaders not for position, but for their faithful labor in the gospel.

6. Choose one specific way to encourage a leader this week: through a note, a prayer, or personal service, fulfilling the law of Christ through love.

Introduction:

If you've ever served in leadership, as an elder, deacon, teacher, preacher, or ministry worker, you understand that the work is both joyful and heavy. Leaders carry the spiritual weight of shepherding people, often dealing with challenges and criticism that others never see. They are called to "keep watch over souls" (Hebrews 13:17), a responsibility that demands both strength and humility. Yet leaders are also human. They get tired, discouraged, and sometimes feel unseen.

That's why the Bible repeatedly calls God's people to honor, support, and encourage their leaders. Hebrews 13:7 reminds us to *remember your leaders who have spoken God's word to you* and to *imitate their faith.* Verse 17 adds that we should obey and submit to them *so that they can do this with joy and not with grief.* And in 1 Thessalonians 5:12–13, Paul urges Christians to *recognize those who labor among you and are over you in the Lord* and to *regard them very highly in love because of their work.*

Leadership in the church is a sacred trust, and it thrives in an atmosphere of gratitude and love. When leaders are encouraged, the whole church is strengthened. When leaders are constantly criticized or left unsupported, the entire body suffers.

In this lesson, we'll explore what it means to follow godly leaders, how to support them joyfully, and how to show love in ways that refresh their hearts. Encouraging leaders is a spiritual responsibility that reflects the heart of Christ Himself, who shepherded with compassion, patience, and grace.

Remember and Follow Godly Leaders

The writer of Hebrews begins his exhortation by saying, *...remember your leaders who have spoken God's word to you. As you carefully observe the outcome of their lives, imitate their faith,* Hebrews 13:7.

That one verse captures three simple but powerful responsibilities for every Christian: **remember**, **observe**, and **imitate**.

1. Remember Their Work

To "remember" here doesn't just mean to think fondly of leaders who have influenced us; it means to keep their example close to mind. These are the men who taught us the Word of God, prayed for us, counseled us, and helped shape our walk with Christ. Their sacrifices often go unseen, long hours of study, countless visits, difficult conversations, and emotional investment in the lives of others. Encouragement begins with gratitude, remembering that leaders serve not for applause, but because they love the Lord and His people.

2. Observe Their Faithfulness

The verse continues, ...as *you carefully observe the outcome of their lives.* The word *observe* means to look attentively to study closely. We're to watch not just what our leaders say, but how they live. Authentic leadership is verified by consistency: by the evidence of faith under pressure, humility in success, and endurance in trial. A godly leader's life is an open book that teaches long after the sermon ends.

I remember an elder in one congregation who spent hours visiting and spending time with those in the local church, often without anyone knowing. He mentored one of our teens by taking him fishing. When he passed away, story after story surfaced at his funeral about quiet acts of service he'd done. People didn't just remember what he said; they remembered *how* he lived. His example continues to shape lives even after his passing.

3. Imitate Their Faith

The command ends with, *imitate their faith.* We are not called to imitate their personalities or preferences, but their faith, their trust in God, their perseverance in hardship, and their devotion to the truth. The greatest tribute we can give to a faithful leader is not applause, but imitation. When we carry forward their example of integrity, humility, and service, we honor both them and Christ, whom they follow.

Practically, this means taking time to reflect on the people who have helped form your faith. Who taught you Scripture when you were young? Who encouraged you when you were struggling? Who modeled prayer, patience, or courage? Thank God for them and then strive to walk in the same faith.

Encouraging leaders begins here: with gratitude for their work, respect for their example, and a heart determined to follow their faith. Remembering their sacrifices keeps us humble; imitating their faith keeps the church strong.

Support and Submit to Leadership

The writer of Hebrews continues, *...obey your leaders and submit to them, since they keep watch over your souls as those who will give an account, so that they can do this with joy and not with grief, for that would be unprofitable for you,* Hebrews 13:17.

This verse can feel counter-cultural in a world that resists authority and prizes independence. Yet the principle here is not about blind obedience; it's about mutual trust, respect, and cooperation within the family of God. Church leadership is not domination; it's stewardship. Elders and spiritual leaders are shepherds who serve under the Chief Shepherd, Jesus Christ (1 Peter 5:2–4). And those who follow are called to do so with humility and a cooperative spirit that strengthens the whole body.

1. The Role of Leadership: Watching Over Souls

The writer reminds us that leaders "keep watch over your souls." This phrase describes the constant vigilance of a shepherd who stays alert at night, guarding his flock from danger. True spiritual leaders are not managing an organization; they are protecting eternal souls. They pray for the flock, guide it through hardship, and sometimes confront when sin threatens to destroy. That is a sacred and heavy responsibility.

Good leaders don't seek control; they seek care. They will one day "give an account" to God for how they watched over the souls entrusted to them. Imagine the weight of that calling. It's one thing to lead a company or manage a team; it's another to shepherd the souls of men and women created in the image of God.

2. The Responsibility of the Flock: Obedience and Submission

Paul's words, *obey your leaders and submit to them,* are rooted in the idea of willing cooperation, not forced compliance. Submission here means to *yield,* to recognize, and support the God-given role of those who lead. It's the same kind of submission we practice in other biblical relationships, between spouses, between citizens and governing authorities, between Christians and Christ. It's an act of faith, trusting that God works through His appointed servants.

When members refuse to follow godly leadership, tension and division arise. But when the church works together in harmony, leaders serving selflessly and members following faithfully, the result is joy. That's why the verse says, *so that they can do this with joy and not with grief.* Leaders who serve among cooperative, supportive believers are encouraged to lead with renewed energy. But when they face constant resistance, criticism, or apathy, their work becomes heavy and the whole church suffers.

3. The Benefit for Everyone: Growth and Unity

The writer concludes, *for that would be unprofitable for you.* In other words, when leaders lead joyfully and members follow faithfully, everyone benefits. The church grows stronger, unity deepens, and spiritual progress accelerates. But when leadership becomes a constant struggle, the energy that should go toward evangelism, teaching, and care is drained by internal conflict.

Practically, supporting leadership means:

- Praying for your elders, deacons, and teachers regularly.
- Speaking encouragement more than criticism.
- Giving them the benefit of the doubt when decisions are hard.
- Protecting their reputation from gossip.
- Following their example in faith and love.

When leaders are supported, they lead better. When they lead better, the church flourishes. The way we treat our leaders says much about how we view the Lord who appointed them.

Esteem and Encourage Leaders in Love

In 1 Thessalonians 5:12–13, Paul writes, *now we ask you, brothers and sisters, to give recognition to those who labor among you and lead you in the Lord and admonish you, and to regard them very highly in love because of their work. Be at peace among yourselves.* These verses form one of the most beautiful pictures of the relationship between church leaders and members in all of Scripture. Paul gives three key instructions: **recognize, esteem, and love.**

1. Recognize Their Work

Paul begins with the phrase, *...give recognition to those who labor among you.* The word "labor" here means to toil to the point of exhaustion. Authentic leadership in the church is not about status; it's about sacrifice. Elders, preachers, and servants often labor quietly behind the scenes: counseling the broken, visiting the sick, making difficult decisions, and bearing spiritual burdens that few ever see. Paul urges the church: *Don't overlook their labor. Acknowledge it. Appreciate it. Thank God for it.*

Encouragement begins with awareness. We can't appreciate what we never notice. That's why Paul calls us to recognize their effort and devotion.

2. Esteem Them in Love

Next, Paul says, *regard them very highly in love because of their work.* This is heartfelt affection. The phrase "very highly" means to go beyond the usual measure. In other words, let love overflow toward those who serve. We don't honor leaders because they're perfect (no one is); we honor them because of the love and labor they pour out for the sake of Christ and His people.

Genuine esteem for leaders is rooted in *love*, not flattery. It shows up in prayer, gratitude, and acts of kindness. It's the note of appreciation, the handshake after worship, the offer to help lighten their load. Small gestures of love carry immense weight for those who often carry heavy responsibilities. Leaders frequently serve quietly, rarely hearing affirmation unless something goes wrong. Paul's instruction challenges us to change that pattern, to be intentional about expressing love and gratitude often.

3. Protect Unity and Peace

Paul ends this section with a simple command: *be at peace among yourselves.* Encouragement of leaders and unity in the church go hand in hand. A congregation that loves and esteems its leaders will naturally be a place of peace. When people speak kindly, serve willingly, and follow faithfully, tension fades and love abounds.

When leaders feel supported, they can lead with joy, and when they lead with joy, the whole church benefits. The reverse is also true: when leaders are constantly under criticism, the spirit of the church is weakened. Encouragement is not only a gift to leaders; it's a blessing to the entire body.

Practically, this means:

- Express gratitude often: verbally, in writing, or through service.
- Guard your leaders' hearts by refusing to participate in gossip or negativity.
- Look for ways to help share their load.
- Encourage their families, who also bear the weight of ministry.

Paul's closing phrase, *because of their work,* reminds us that appreciation isn't based on personality or preference, but on faithfulness. When we honor those who lead us in the Lord, we honor the Lord who appointed them.

Practical Application: How to Encourage Leaders

Encouraging spiritual leaders isn't complicated, but it is intentional. Small acts of support and love can make a lasting difference in the life of an elder, deacon, preacher, teacher, or servant who labors for the Lord. Here are some practical ways to put this lesson into action:

1. **Pray for Your Leaders Daily**
   Leaders need wisdom, courage, and endurance. Paul often asked believers to pray for him "that the word of the Lord may spread rapidly" (2 Thessalonians 3:1) and for boldness and strength

(Ephesians 6:19). Prayer is the most powerful encouragement we can offer. Keep your leaders' names on your daily prayer list—not just in times of crisis, but consistently.

2. **Express Gratitude Regularly**
   Write a note, send a message, or say a simple "thank you." Let your elders, deacons, preachers, and teachers know that their labor is making a difference. Be specific: mention a moment when their teaching, decision, or compassion blessed you. Words of gratitude have lasting power.
3. **Offer Practical Support**
   Encouragement isn't just spoken, it's shown. Offer to help with tasks, take something off their plate, or volunteer for a need they're managing. When you step up to serve, you not only lighten their load but also affirm their leadership.
4. **Refuse Gossip or Criticism**
   Few things discourage leaders more than constant criticism or gossip. If you hear unkind talk, stop it or redirect it toward prayer. Protect your leaders' reputation the way you'd want others to protect yours. Unity and encouragement grow where love governs speech.
5. **Encourage Their Families**
   Leadership often places unique demands on spouses and children. Take time to encourage them, too, through kindness, understanding, and prayer. A strong family strengthens the servant who leads.
6. **Follow Faithfully and Joyfully**
   Hebrews 13:17 reminds us that leaders should be able to serve "with joy and not with grief." When members cooperate, communicate, and participate with love, leaders are refreshed. The most encouraging gift a church can give its leaders is joyful unity and willing service.

Challenge

This week, choose one leader (an elder, deacon, teacher, or ministry servant) and do something tangible to encourage them. Write a note, offer to help, pray with them, or thank them for their faithfulness. Then, commit to praying daily for all your leaders this month.

Conclusion

Strong leadership is one of God's greatest blessings to a congregation, but it's also one of the heaviest burdens. Elders, deacons, preachers, and teachers give of themselves day after day, often quietly and sacrificially, watching over souls and guiding hearts. Their work is vital, but their strength is not unlimited. That's why Scripture calls us, the church, to stand beside them, pray for them, and make their work a joy, not a grief.

We've learned that encouragement begins by **remembering** those who have spoken the Word to us and **imitating their faith** (Hebrews 13:7). It continues as we **support and submit** to them, recognizing that they watch over our souls as those who will give an account (Hebrews 13:17). And it grows as we **esteem them highly in love** for their labor (1 Thessalonians 5:12–13).

Encouraging leaders is not about flattery or favoritism; it's about faithfulness. It's about honoring God by honoring those who serve Him well. When we pray for our leaders, speak kindly of them, and help share their load, we strengthen the entire church. A joyful leader inspires a joyful congregation; a supported shepherd leads a healthy flock.

Look for ways this week to bless those who lead you in the Lord. Send that note. Offer that prayer. Speak that word of gratitude. Stand beside them in love and unity. When you do, you're not just encouraging a leader; you're fulfilling the law of Christ and helping the whole body grow in grace and peace.

For Discussion

1. Who has been a spiritual leader or mentor in your life who deeply influenced your faith? What specific things did they do that made their leadership meaningful?

   ____

   ____

   ____

2. Why does the writer of Hebrews connect remembering leaders with imitating their faith? What does this teach us about the kind of example spiritual leadership should set in the church?

___

___

___

3. What are some practical ways we can make our leaders' work "a joy and not a grief"? How does our attitude toward leadership affect the unity and health of the congregation?

___

___

___

4. Paul urges us to "regard them very highly in love because of their work." Why is love a key part of honoring and encouraging leaders, and what might that look like in daily congregational life?

___

___

___

5. What sometimes prevents members from encouraging or supporting their leaders? How can we overcome criticism, misunderstanding, or apathy in order to build up those who serve?

___

___

___

6. What's one concrete step you can take this week to encourage a leader—whether through prayer, service, or words of appreciation? How could your example inspire others to do the same?

___

___

___

Part Three

Endurance Tools

The work of ministry requires perseverance. Service to Christ often encounters trials, opposition, and the temptation to grow weary. In this section, we will focus on the endurance tools that sustain faith and strengthen commitment: persevering through trials, standing firm in truth and grace, working together in unity, and bringing all the tools of ministry into practice. These disciplines equip us not only to remain steadfast in the face of hardship but also to continue building up the body of Christ with resilience and hope.

Lesson 9

How to Handle Conflict Biblically

Matthew 18:15–17; Ephesians 4:1–3

If your brother sins against you, go tell him his fault, between you and him alone. If he listens to you, you have won your brother. But if he won't listen, take one or two others with you, so that by the testimony of two or three witnesses every fact may be established. If he doesn't pay attention to them, tell the church. If he doesn't pay attention even to the church, let him be like a Gentile and a tax collector to you, Matthew 18:15–17.

Class Overview: Conflict is an unavoidable part of life, even within the church. But while conflict is inevitable, division is not. Jesus taught His followers in *Matthew 18:15–17* how to address disagreements with humility and truth, beginning privately and aiming always for restoration. Paul reinforces this in *Ephesians 4:1–3*, reminding believers that peace requires effort, patience, and love. The goal of biblical conflict resolution is not to win arguments but to win hearts, to preserve unity and strengthen relationships within the body of Christ. When we handle conflict with grace, we reveal the transforming power of the gospel and protect the unity of the Spirit that binds us together.

Class Objectives:

By the end of this class, you should be able to:

1. Explain the three key steps of Matthew 18:15–17 and how they protect relationships from gossip and division.
2. Describe how humility, gentleness, patience, and love (Ephesians 4:1–3) are essential to keeping unity in times of tension.
3. Identify practical ways to approach disagreements in personal and congregational life with truth and grace.
4. Understand when and how to involve others in conflict resolution, and why wise, godly mediators strengthen the church.
5. Commit to releasing resentment and extending mercy as Christ has forgiven us (Colossians 3:13)

6. Commit to being a peacemaker in every relationship, remembering that restored fellowship glorifies Christ and strengthens His church.

Introduction:

Years ago, I remember a disagreement between members in our congregation over how many times to serve the Lord's Supper on Sunday. What started as a misunderstanding in a business meeting quickly grew into frustration, and within a few weeks, people in the church were avoiding each other entirely. Throughout the summer, the congregation studied the issue. By the fall, things had been worked out and peace restored. I've never forgotten those months because they illustrated one of the most essential truths about relationships in the church: most conflicts don't require big interventions; they just require honest conversations.

Conflict is a part of life, even in the family of God. Wherever there are people, there will be differences: differences in opinion, personality, and perception. But conflict itself isn't the problem; how we handle it is. If ignored or mishandled, minor disagreements can grow into division. But when handled with humility and love, conflict becomes an opportunity for growth, grace, and stronger relationships.

Jesus understood this, which is why He gave clear, practical instructions for how to resolve conflict among believers. In Matthew 18:15–17, He outlines a process rooted in love and truth: a pattern that protects relationships and preserves unity. And Paul teaches this in Ephesians 4:1–3, urging Christians to "walk worthy of the calling you have received, with all humility and gentleness, with patience, bearing with one another in love, making every effort to keep the unity of the Spirit through the bond of peace."

The goal of conflict resolution isn't to prove we're right; it's to keep relationships right. It's not to win an argument, it's to win a brother or sister back.

So today, as we study how to handle conflict biblically, we'll look at three simple but powerful principles from Scripture: confront privately, seek help when needed, and pursue peace through humility. When we follow these steps, we turn moments of tension into opportunities for spiritual maturity, and the church becomes a living reflection of Christ's grace and unity.

Confront Privately and Humbly

In Matthew 18:15, Jesus said, *if your brother sins against you, go and rebuke him in private. If he listens to you, you have won your brother.* This verse lays out the first and most essential step in handling conflict biblically: go to the person directly, privately, and with humility. In our culture, it's far easier to talk *about* someone than to talk *to* them. But Jesus reverses that instinct. He commands us to face problems head-on: not to embarrass, accuse, or shame, but to restore.

The goal of confrontation, in Jesus' words, is not to prove who's right, but to *win your brother.* That phrase captures the heart of Christian reconciliation. It's not about scoring a victory; it's about preserving a relationship when we remember that the person who hurt us is not our enemy but our brother or sister in Christ, everything about our tone, attitude, and purpose changes.

1. Go Directly, Not Publicly

Notice that Jesus says to go "in private." He doesn't say to post about it, complain to a friend, or bring it before the church. The first step is a one-on-one conversation. Why? Because love protects. Private correction guards dignity, minimizes embarrassment, and allows for honesty. Most conflicts can be resolved quietly if handled this way. When we involve others prematurely, we risk damaging reputations and deepening division.

Think about how you'd want to be approached if you had unknowingly offended someone. Wouldn't you want the chance to make it right privately before it became public? Jesus' wisdom protects that opportunity.

2. Go Humbly, Not Harshly

Jesus says, *go and rebuke him,* but the word "rebuke" here means to point out gently, not to attack. The spirit of confrontation should be one of humility, not hostility. Galatians 6:1 says: *If someone is overtaken in any wrongdoing, you who are spiritual, restore such a person with a gentle spirit.* The aim is restoration, not humiliation.

Before you go, pray. Ask God to search your heart (Psalm 139:23–24). Make sure your goal is reconciliation, not retaliation. If your motivation is to prove a point or demand an apology, your heart isn't ready. But if you desire to bring peace and healing, God can use that conversation powerfully.

3. Go to Restore, Not to Relieve

It's easy to confront others to "get it off our chest." But Jesus wants more than emotional relief; He wants relational restoration. The end goal is that you "win your brother." When conflict is handled biblically, both sides grow in grace, humility, and mutual respect.

Here's a simple rule: if you're not willing to pray for the person, you're not ready to confront the person. Conflict handled in prayerful humility often ends in peace; conflict handled in pride almost never does.

Practically, this means that when tension arises, you don't delay indefinitely, but you also don't rush in angry. Take the initiative to go privately, with grace in your heart and love in your tone. Ask questions instead of making accusations. Listen more than you speak. Sometimes the very act of approaching someone kindly breaks down the walls of misunderstanding.

Jesus knew that unresolved conflict destroys unity. That's why He gave us this clear path: go privately, go humbly, go to win your brother. If every believer practiced this one verse, the vast majority of church conflicts would disappear overnight.

Seek Help When Needed

After explaining that reconciliation begins privately, Jesus adds, *but if he won't listen, take one or two others with you, so that by the testimony of two or three witnesses every fact may be established. If he doesn't pay attention to them, tell the church. If he doesn't pay attention even to the church, let him be like a Gentile and a tax collector to you.* These verses remind us that while most conflicts can be resolved one-on-one, some require help. Jesus gives a straightforward, step-by-step process for how to involve others in a way that promotes accountability and unity, not gossip or shame.

1. Bring in Wise, Objective Help

Jesus says to bring "one or two others." Not everyone you can find, but trusted, spiritually mature believers who can listen objectively and help mediate. Their presence ensures fairness and clarity. Sometimes emotions cloud our perception, and an outside perspective brings balance and peace.

The purpose of involving others is not to "gang up" on the other person but to verify facts and encourage repentance and reconciliation. It's a loving safeguard that prevents misunderstandings and keeps the process anchored in truth.

In 2021, engineers made a startling discovery on the I–40 bridge that spans the Mississippi River between Memphis, Tennessee, and West Memphis, Arkansas. During a routine inspection, they found a massive crack in one of the bridge's main support beams. It wasn't a minor flaw; it was a fracture large enough to threaten the safety of everyone crossing it. Immediately, the bridge was shut down. Traffic stopped. Experts from around the country were called in. The goal wasn't demolition, it was *repair.* Engineers worked carefully to stabilize the structure, reinforce the damaged section, and restore the bridge to full strength. It took time, precision, and teamwork. Eventually, the bridge reopened; not weaker, but stronger than before.

That's a perfect picture of what Jesus describes in Matthew 18:16–17. When relationships crack under tension, the goal isn't to tear them down; it's to repair them. And sometimes, just like with that bridge, we need help from others who can stabilize the structure. Wise, godly mediators come alongside not to take sides or assign blame, but to strengthen what's broken.

When a relationship is strained, emotions run high, and perspective can be lost. That's when mature Christians, elders, ministers, or trusted friends act like those engineers on the bridge. They bring steadiness, wisdom, and patience. They help both sides see clearly, understand the truth, and rebuild trust. Their goal isn't demolition, it's restoration. Their presence doesn't widen the crack; it helps seal it. And when handled with grace, the relationship that once seemed fragile can emerge stronger, more honest, and more Christlike than before.

2. Protect the Church from Division

If the conflict still cannot be resolved, Jesus says to "tell it to the church." This step isn't about public humiliation; it's about protecting the integrity of the body. When persistent sin or hardened hearts threaten unity, the church must lovingly intervene to call for repentance. The goal is always restoration, never exclusion.

Even in the final phrase, *let him be like a Gentile and a tax collector to you,* Jesus doesn't instruct hatred or hostility. Remember how Jesus Himself treated Gentiles and tax collectors: with truth, compassion, and a desire for redemption. This final step acknowledges broken fellowship but still leaves the door open for grace.

3. Keep the Focus on Restoration, Not Punishment

At every stage, the goal remains the same: to win your brother. If the first conversation doesn't work, try again with help. If the second fails, bring it before the church. But through it all, keep the spirit of humility, gentleness, and love. The process Jesus outlines protects relationships, guards the church's witness, and ensures that truth and grace remain in balance.

Conflict escalates when we skip steps, when we talk to everyone *except* the person involved, or when we go public before we go private. But when we follow Jesus' pattern, even difficult situations can lead to healing.

Practically, this means that when conflict persists, seek help from godly people, elders, ministers, or spiritually mature members, who can guide the conversation toward peace. Invite wisdom, not opinion. Ask others to pray with you, not gossip with you. The presence of others should always make reconciliation more likely, not less. When handled correctly, involving mature believers can turn stubborn tension into humble restoration.

Pursue Peace through Humility

After giving practical instructions for conflict resolution, Paul reminds believers of the spirit that must undergird it all: *therefore I, the prisoner in the Lord, urge you to walk worthy of the calling you have received, with all humility and gentleness, with patience, bearing with one another in love, making every effort to keep the unity of the Spirit through the bond of peace,* Ephesians 4:1–3. Conflict resolution is not just a process; it's a posture. Even when we follow all the proper steps, reconciliation will fail if pride or anger rules our hearts. That's why Paul begins with *walk worthy of the calling you have received.* How we handle conflict reflects the gospel we proclaim.

1. Walk Worthy of Your Calling

To "walk worthy" means to live in a manner that reflects Christ. The gospel calls us to peace because Christ Himself is our peace (Ephesians 2:14). The way we respond to disagreement either honors or hinders that calling. When believers handle conflict with grace and truth, the church's unity becomes a living testimony to the power of the gospel. Conflict handled poorly pushes people away; conflict handled biblically draws people closer, not just to each other, but to Christ.

2. Embrace the Posture of Humility and Gentleness

Paul names four attitudes essential for keeping peace: humility, gentleness, patience, and love. These are not natural reactions; they are spiritual disciplines formed by the Spirit.

- **Humility** means letting go of pride and the need to be right.
- **Gentleness** means using words that heal instead of harm.
- **Patience** means giving others time and grace to change.
- **Love** means valuing the relationship more than the argument.

Think about a skilled surgeon operating on a wound. The goal is to remove what's harmful without causing further injury. That requires precision, patience, and care; not haste or harshness. In the same way, when we address conflict with humility and gentleness, we help heal the wound without creating new ones.

3. Make Every Effort to Keep Unity

Paul emphasizes *making every effort to maintain the unity of the Spirit.* Remember, unity is not something we create; it's something we *preserve.* God has already established unity through the Spirit; our role is to guard it. This means that conflict is not an interruption of ministry; it *is* part of ministry. The way we respond during moments of tension either protects or disrupts what the Spirit has built.

Unity requires effort, sometimes uncomfortable effort. It means we keep showing up, keep forgiving, keep talking, and keep loving, even when it's hard. The phrase "bond of peace" suggests something that ties us together; the glue of grace that keeps the body from coming apart.

Practically, this means practicing humility in every conflict. Before speaking, pray. Before reacting, listen. Before assuming, ask questions. Before condemning, remember how much patience God has shown you. When humility leads and love guides, peace follows. Paul's vision of unity is not the absence of disagreement but the presence of grace. The church is at its strongest not when everyone always agrees, but when everyone agrees to handle disagreement in a Christlike way.

Practical Application: How to Handle Conflict Biblically

Handling conflict God's way is rarely easy. But it is always worth it. The steps Jesus outlines in Matthew 18 and the attitude Paul describes in Ephesians 4 show us that peace doesn't happen by accident; it occurs through humility, patience, and obedience. Here are some practical ways to apply these principles this week:

1. **Pray Before You Speak**
   Before addressing any conflict, stop and pray. Ask God to search your heart (Psalm 139:23–24) and purify your motives. Ask for wisdom, gentleness, and courage. Prayer softens pride and prepares your heart to listen instead of reacting.
2. **Go to the Person, Not Around Them**
   Follow Jesus' words in Matthew 18:15. Talk privately and directly to the person involved: not to others. Avoid gossip, group chats, or

"venting." The shortest route to reconciliation is still face-to-face.

3. **Listen to Understand, Not to Win**
   In conflict, it's easy to prepare your defense instead of opening your ears. James 1:19 says, *everyone should be quick to listen, slow to speak, and slow to anger.* Ask questions like, "Can you help me understand what you meant?" Listening communicates respect and often reveals that misunderstandings, not malice, lie at the heart of the problem.
4. **Speak the Truth in Love**
   Ephesians 4:15 calls us to speak truth lovingly. That means being honest without being harsh. Avoid exaggeration or blame. Use "I" statements instead of "you" accusations ("I felt hurt when ..." rather than "You always ..."). Truth heals when it's wrapped in grace.
5. **Involve Wise Help When Needed**
   If resolution doesn't come, bring one or two spiritually mature believers into the conversation (Matthew 18:16). Their goal isn't to take sides, but to bring balance, peace, and accountability. Choose people known for discretion and wisdom, not for drama or opinions.
6. **Forgive Freely and Quickly**
   Conflict can only heal when forgiveness flows. Colossians 3:13 says, *Just as the Lord has forgiven you, so you are also to forgive.* Forgiveness doesn't always mean forgetting, but it does mean releasing resentment. When you forgive, you imitate Christ and free both your heart and the relationship.
7. **Keep the Relationship the Goal**
   The aim of conflict resolution is not to win the argument but to win your brother or sister. Remember, unity is the Spirit's work; your job is to protect it (Ephesians 4:3). When love leads and humility follows, peace becomes possible.

Challenge

This week, examine your relationships. Is there someone with whom tension exists—a misunderstanding, hurt, or silent distance? Pray for courage and grace, then take the first step to reach out. Have the conversation. Be the bridge-builder. Choose restoration over resentment and unity over pride.

Conclusion

Conflict is inevitable, but division is optional. Every disagreement we face, whether small or serious, is an opportunity to either reflect the character of Christ or the pride of the world. The way we handle tension reveals the depth of our faith. Jesus never promised that relationships would be free of conflict, but He did show us how to face it with grace, truth, and love.

In Matthew 18, He gave us a simple, God-honoring process: go privately, involve others when needed, and keep the goal of restoration at the center. And in *Ephesians 4*, Paul reminds us that the spirit behind every step must be humility, gentleness, patience, and love. When we follow these commands, peace becomes possible, not because everyone agrees on everything, but because everyone agrees to honor Christ above everything.

The truth is that broken relationships damage more than feelings; they damage the witness of the church. But when believers humble themselves, seek forgiveness, and reconcile, the world sees something powerful: a people transformed by grace. Jesus said, *blessed are the peacemakers, for they will be called sons of God* (Matthew 5:9).

If there's tension between you and someone else, take the first step this week. Pray. Reach out. Talk honestly. Forgive freely. Choose unity over pride. Every healed relationship strengthens the church and glorifies Christ, the Prince of Peace. When we handle conflict biblically, we don't just resolve problems; we reveal the gospel.

For Discussion

1. Can you think of a time when a conflict in your life or in the church was resolved peacefully and biblically? What attitudes or actions helped bring about that resolution?

   ____

   ____

   ____

2. Why do you think Jesus emphasizes handling conflict privately first? How might following this step prevent gossip, division, or unnecessary hurt?

____

____

____

3. What kind of people should be involved when conflict can't be resolved one-on-one? How does involving wise, godly mediators protect relationships and unity?

____

____

____

4. Paul lists humility, gentleness, patience, and love as essential for unity. Which of these is most difficult for you to practice in moments of conflict, and why?

____

____

____

5. Why is forgiveness so vital to resolving conflict? What happens to relationships, and to your own spiritual health, when you withhold forgiveness?

____

____

____

6. Is there someone you need to reach out to this week to repair a strained relationship? What step will you take first: prayer, conversation, or forgiveness, to begin the process of reconciliation?

____

____

____

Lesson 10

How to Forgive and Move Forward

Colossians 3:12–14; Matthew 6:14–15

For if you forgive others their offenses, your heavenly Father will forgive you as well. But if you don't forgive others, your Father will not forgive your offenses, Matthew 6:14–15.

Therefore, as God's chosen ones, holy and dearly loved, put on compassion, kindness, humility, gentleness, and patience, bearing with one another and forgiving one another if anyone has a grievance against another. Just as the Lord has forgiven you, so you are also to forgive. Above all, put on love, which is the perfect bond of unity, Colossians 3:12–14.

Class Overview: Forgiveness lies at the very heart of the Christian faith. It is both a command and a calling—an imitation of the mercy God has shown us through Christ. In *Colossians 3:12–14* and *Matthew 6:14–15*, we learn that forgiveness is not optional for believers; it is the natural response of those who have experienced grace. Unforgiveness traps us in bitterness, while forgiveness releases us into freedom and peace. Through forgiveness, we reflect God's character, restore broken fellowship, and rebuild love within the body of Christ. This lesson calls believers to lay down resentment, trust God with justice, and move forward in mercy, allowing His grace to heal what has been broken.

Class Objectives:

By the end of this class, you should be able to:

1. Explain how forgiveness is rooted in God's nature and commanded for all believers (Colossians 3:12–13; Matthew 6:14–15).
2. Describe how bitterness hinders our relationship with God and robs us of peace.
3. Identify how forgiving others sets us free from resentment and opens the door to healing.

4. Understand how forgiveness and love work together to rebuild relationships and strengthen the church (Colossians 3:14).
5. Practice daily reflection, prayer, and intentional acts of release as spiritual disciplines of grace.
6. Choose one relationship or situation in need of forgiveness and take a concrete step toward reconciliation or release this week.

Introduction:

Twenty years ago, a couple who were close friends of mine suddenly stopped speaking to me. I wasn't sure why at first. I assumed they were just busy, but over time, I realized something was wrong. Eventually, I learned that a misunderstanding had occurred; something I had said in the pulpit had been misunderstood. By the time I found out, resentment had already taken hold.

For months, I prayed about it, wrestled with what to do, and tried to convince myself that time would fix it. But it didn't. The longer the silence lasted, the heavier the burden became. One day, I finally decided to reach out. We met, talked honestly, and cleared the air. They admitted their hurt. I acknowledged my frustration. Then we prayed together. That day, a friendship was restored, and peace returned to my heart.

Forgiveness is one of the hardest things God asks us to do. It feels unnatural because everything in us wants to hold onto the hurt, to make the other person pay, or at least to make sure they know how much they've wounded us. Yet Jesus calls us to a higher way, the way of mercy. He teaches us that forgiveness is not optional for the believer; it's essential.

In Colossians 3:12–13, Paul reminds us, *as God's chosen ones, holy and dearly loved, put on compassion, kindness, humility, gentleness, and patience, bearing with one another and forgiving one another if anyone has a grievance against another. Just as the Lord has forgiven you, so you are also to forgive.* That last line stops us in our tracks: *Just as the Lord has forgiven you.*

Forgiveness is not based on what someone else deserves; it's based on what we've received. Every time we forgive, we're simply passing along what God has already given to us. And when we refuse to forgive, we cut ourselves off from the very grace that saved us. Jesus said in Matthew 6:14–15, *if you forgive others their offenses, your heavenly Father will forgive you as well. But if you don't forgive others, your Father will not forgive your offenses.* Unforgiveness is a prison, one that keeps both hearts locked inside. But forgiveness? It's freedom. It releases us from the weight of bitterness and opens the door to healing, restoration, and renewed love.

Today, we're going to explore what forgiveness really means, not as a theory, but as a way of life. We'll see that forgiveness reflects God's character, restores our freedom, and rebuilds our relationships. And by the end of this lesson, my prayer is that you'll see forgiveness not as a painful obligation, but as a powerful opportunity to reflect the grace of God and move forward in peace.

Forgiveness Reflects God's Character

In Colossians 3:12–14, Paul writes, *therefore, as God's chosen ones, holy and dearly loved, put on compassion, kindness, humility, gentleness, and patience, bearing with one another and forgiving one another if anyone has a grievance against another. Just as the Lord has forgiven you, so you are also to forgive.*

Forgiveness begins with remembering who we are, and whose we are. Paul reminds us that we are *God's chosen ones, holy and dearly loved.* Those three truths form the foundation of forgiveness:

- We forgive because we belong to God.
- We forgive because we've been set apart by His grace.
- We forgive because we are deeply loved by Him.

When we understand that, forgiveness stops being an emotional reaction and becomes an act of imitation. We forgive because it's what our Father does.

1. Forgiveness Flows from Compassion and Kindness

Paul tells us to "put on" compassion, kindness, humility, gentleness, and patience. These virtues are like the clothing of Christ, what we wear as His people. Forgiveness is what happens when those virtues come together. Compassion sees the person behind the offense. Kindness softens the words that could wound further. Humility admits that we, too, need grace. Gentleness chooses restoration over retaliation. Patience gives time for healing. Forgiveness doesn't mean pretending that wrong didn't happen; it means responding to it with the heart of Christ.

2. Forgiveness Imitates God's Grace

The phrase *just as the Lord has forgiven you* is both a reminder and a standard. God didn't forgive us because we earned it. He forgave us because of His mercy. Romans 5:8 says, *while we were still sinners, Christ died for us.* If God could forgive us at our worst, how can we withhold forgiveness from others at theirs? Forgiveness is not about keeping score; it's about keeping grace in motion. Every time you forgive, you're continuing the work God began in you. You become a living reflection of His mercy to the world.

Think of a mirror. Its only purpose is to reflect what shines upon it. When God's grace shines on a forgiven heart, it's meant to reflect that grace outward. But if the mirror is covered with dust: resentment, bitterness, pride, the reflection fades. Forgiveness wipes the surface clean so that God's love can shine through you again.

3. Forgiveness Honors Our Identity in Christ

Paul's command to forgive is not a burden; it's a privilege. It's the mark of the mature believer who knows what it means to be forgiven much. The more we grow in our awareness of God's mercy toward us, the more willing we become to extend that mercy to others.

Practically, this means that forgiveness isn't optional; it's essential to discipleship. If I belong to Christ, then I must reflect His character. That means refusing to let bitterness define me. It means choosing to forgive, even when my emotions scream otherwise. It means letting grace have the final word.

When you forgive, you are doing one of the most Godlike things a human being can do. You're showing the world what divine love looks like in human form. Forgiveness is not weakness, it's strength under control, power wrapped in mercy.

Forgiveness Restores Our Freedom

Jesus says something both beautiful and sobering in the Sermon on the Mount: *for if you forgive others their offenses, your heavenly Father will forgive you as well. But if you don't forgive others, your Father will not forgive your offenses.*

These words follow immediately after the Lord's Prayer, right after Jesus taught His disciples to say, *forgive us our debts, as we also have forgiven our debtors.* The connection is intentional. Jesus wants us to see that forgiveness is not only something we *receive*; it's something we *extend.* We cannot live in the freedom of God's grace while holding others captive in our bitterness.

1. Unforgiveness Is a Prison

Bitterness promises control; it tells us that if we hold onto the hurt, we'll somehow regain power over what was lost. But unforgiveness doesn't imprison the offender; it imprisons the offended. It keeps us tied to the pain of the past. Every time we replay the offense, the chain tightens a little more.

Jesus' warning in verse 15 is not about losing salvation; it's about losing intimacy with God. When we refuse to forgive, we close our hearts to the very mercy we need. We cannot ask God to pour out grace on us while we withhold it from others.

There's an old story about two monks who came to a river. A woman stood nearby, unable to cross. One monk picked her up and carried her across, setting her down on the other side. Hours later, as they walked in silence, the other monk finally said, "I can't believe you carried that woman, it was against our rules!" The first monk replied, "Brother, I put her down hours ago, but you're still carrying her." Unforgiveness works the same way. It keeps us carrying what Christ has already given us permission to set down.

2. Forgiveness Releases the Weight of the Past

When we forgive, we are not excusing sin; we are releasing ourselves from its control. Forgiveness doesn't mean saying, "It didn't hurt," it means saying, "It no longer controls me." It's choosing freedom over bondage, healing over hatred.

Ephesians 4:31–32 reveals this truth: *let all bitterness, anger, and wrath, shouting and slander be removed from you, along with all malice. And be kind and compassionate to one another, forgiving one another, just as God also forgave you in Christ.* Notice that forgiveness is paired with kindness and compassion: two attitudes that create space for peace to grow again.

3. Forgiveness Renews Fellowship with God

Jesus ties our forgiveness of others directly to our fellowship with the Father. When we forgive, we reopen the channels of grace in our hearts. Prayer becomes richer. Worship becomes freer. The peace of God, which passes understanding, retakes root.

Unforgiveness, on the other hand, makes spiritual life feel dry and distant. It's hard to draw near to God when bitterness is standing in the way. But when we release resentment, we make room for His presence to fill us again. Practically, this means forgiveness is not a one-time decision; it's a daily commitment. Some wounds take time to heal, and forgiveness may need to be renewed again and again. But every time you choose to forgive, you loosen the grip of the past and strengthen the grip of grace. Forgiveness doesn't erase memory; it redeems it. It turns the story of hurt into a testimony of healing. It restores freedom not only to the one who hurt you but to your own heart as well.

Forgiveness Rebuilds Relationships

Paul concludes his beautiful section on Christian character with this statement: *above all, put on love, which is the perfect bond of unity.* In other words, love is what ties everything together. Compassion, kindness, humility, patience, and forgiveness all find their completeness in love. Without love, forgiveness becomes mechanical, an obligation rather than a transformation. But when love rules the heart, forgiveness flows naturally.

1. Love Is the Glue That Holds Forgiveness Together

Paul uses the phrase *the perfect bond of unity.* The word *bond* comes from a term that means "to bind or tie together." In ancient times, a tailor would stitch multiple pieces of fabric with a single strong thread; that's the picture Paul paints here. Love is the thread that holds the fabric of the church together, even after it's been torn by sin or offense. Forgiveness, then, is the needle God uses to mend what's been ripped apart. It's how love repairs the tears that conflict and hurt create.

2. Forgiveness Opens the Door for Restoration

Forgiveness doesn't always mean the relationship will go back to precisely what it was before. Trust takes time to rebuild. But forgiveness makes restoration possible. It clears the debris of resentment so that love and trust can grow again. Sometimes, the relationship is restored fully. Other times, forgiveness simply means you can look at the person or situation without bitterness, and that's still healing. Either way, forgiveness paves the way for peace. Romans 12:18 reminds us, *if possible, as far as it depends on you, live at peace with everyone.* Forgiveness is your part of that peace. It says, "Even if you don't change, I will no longer let your actions define my heart."

3. Forgiveness Strengthens the Church's Witness

When the world sees believers forgiving one another, it sees something supernatural. In a culture that thrives on revenge, grudges, and canceling others, forgiveness shines like light in darkness. Jesus said in John 13:35, *by this everyone will know that you are My disciples, if you love one another.* Every act of forgiveness within the body of Christ preaches the gospel louder than any sermon. It shows that grace is not just something we talk about; it's something we live.

Practically, rebuilding relationships through forgiveness might mean reaching out again to someone you've avoided. It might mean speaking words of grace instead of criticism. It might mean inviting someone back into your life slowly and prayerfully. But every step toward reconciliation reflects the love of Christ. Forgiveness is how we rebuild what sin tried to destroy. It's how the church becomes a living example of redemption. And it's how believers, once divided, can again walk together in unity and love, bound by the same grace that saved them both.

Practical Application: How to Forgive and Move Forward

Forgiveness is not something we drift into. It is a decision we make, often one we must make again and again. It's rarely easy, but it is always freeing. Below are practical steps to help believers move from hurt to healing through the power of God's grace:

1. **Remember What God Has Done for You**
   Every act of forgiveness begins with reflection. Before you focus on what someone has done *to you,* remember what God has done *for you.* We are forgiven sinners, washed clean by the blood of Christ. When we recall the magnitude of our own forgiveness, it becomes harder to cling to resentment. Ephesians 4:32*: be kind and compassionate to one another, forgiving one another, just as God also forgave you in Christ.* Take a few moments in prayer to thank God for His mercy toward you. Forgiveness starts at the foot of the cross.
2. **Acknowledge the Hurt Honestly**
   Forgiveness doesn't mean minimizing pain or pretending it didn't matter. True forgiveness looks pain in the face and chooses to release it. God never asks us to deny our wounds, only to refuse to let them define us. Name the hurt, bring it before the Lord, and then begin the work of letting it go.
3. **Pray for the Person Who Hurt You**
   Jesus said, *love your enemies and pray for those who persecute you* (Matthew 5:44). It's hard to hate someone you're praying for. Even if your heart isn't ready to forgive fully, begin praying anyway. Pray for God's blessing, for their repentance, and for your own healing. Over time, prayer softens resentment and reshapes your heart.
4. **Release the Desire for Revenge**
   Romans 12:19 says, *do not take revenge, dear friends, but leave room for God's wrath.* Forgiveness is an act of trust, entrusting justice to the Lord rather than trying to carry it ourselves. When you forgive, you're not saying the wrong didn't matter; you're saying *you're no longer the judge.* You're placing the situation in the hands of the One who judges righteously.

5. **Choose to Forgive: Even if You Don't Feel Like It**
   Forgiveness is not a feeling; it's a choice of obedience. You may not "feel" forgiving, but you can still *decide* to forgive. Tell God, "I choose to forgive, and I trust You with my emotions." Feelings will follow obedience.
6. **Take One Step Toward Reconciliation**
   Forgiveness opens the door to restored fellowship, but reconciliation takes time. Ask God what your next step should be. Maybe it's writing a note, making a phone call, or simply letting go of bitterness in your heart. Peace begins with one small act of grace.
7. **Keep Forgiving: Until the Heart Is Free**
   Forgiveness may need to be renewed repeatedly. Some wounds resurface when memories return. Each time they do, reaffirm your decision: "I've forgiven this, and I won't pick it back up." Each time you re-release it, the chain grows weaker, and your heart grows lighter.

Challenge

Think of one person who has wronged you, perhaps someone whose name still stirs pain when you hear it. This week, pray for them by name every day. Ask God to help you forgive fully and honestly. Write out a prayer of release, giving that hurt to the Lord once and for all. Then take one small, concrete step toward peace, even if it's simply deciding to stop rehearsing the offense.

Conclusion

Forgiveness is one of the hardest commands in Scripture, but it's also one of the most liberating. It runs against our instincts, yet it aligns perfectly with the heart of God. When we forgive, we are never more like our Father in heaven, who loved us and forgave us when we least deserved it.

Unforgiveness keeps us chained to the past; forgiveness opens the door to the future. It doesn't erase the hurt, but it removes the poison. It doesn't excuse the wrong, but it releases the hold that wrong has over your heart. Through forgiveness, God invites us to trade bitterness for peace, resentment for freedom, and pain for healing.

Paul told the Colossians, *just as the Lord has forgiven you, so you are also to forgive.* That is the standard, and the strength, of Christian forgiveness. We forgive because we've been forgiven. We show mercy because we've been shown mercy. We release others because Christ released us.

Think of the name that still weighs heavily on your heart. Maybe it's someone who hurt you years ago. Perhaps it's a wound that still feels fresh. Today, give that person, and that pain, to God. Say their name out loud in prayer and release the debt. It's not easy, but it's holy.

Forgiveness is not forgetting; it's remembering through the lens of grace. It's choosing to see the cross between you and every wrong that's ever been done to you. And when you do, you'll find that the same grace that saved you is strong enough to set you free.

For Discussion

1. Can you recall a time when someone forgave you deeply or unexpectedly? How did that experience shape your understanding of God's grace?

   ____

   ____

   ____

2. Paul tells us to forgive "just as the Lord has forgiven you." What does this reveal about how forgiveness reflects the heart of God?

   ____

   ____

   ____

3. Why do you think Jesus ties our forgiveness of others to our own relationship with God? How does forgiving others restore freedom and peace in our hearts?

   ____

   ____

   ____

4. Paul says love is the "perfect bond of unity." What role does love play in restoring broken relationships after forgiveness?

   ___

   ___

   ___

5. What makes forgiveness difficult: pride, pain, fear, or something else? How can prayer, perspective, and time help overcome those barriers?

   ___

   ___

   ___

6. Is there someone you need to forgive today—perhaps privately, before God? What specific step will you take this week to move toward release and peace?

   ___

   ___

   ___

Lesson 11

How to Encourage One Another

Hebrews 10:23–25; 1 Thessalonians 5:11

Let us hold on to the confession of our hope without wavering, since he who promised is faithful. And let us consider one another in order to provoke love and good works, not neglecting to gather together, as some are in the habit of doing, but encouraging each other, and all the more as you see the day approaching, Hebrews 10:23–25.

Therefore encourage one another and build each other up as you are already doing, 1 Thessalonians 5:11.

Class Overview: Encouragement is one of the most powerful tools God gives His people to strengthen faith and sustain hope. In Hebrews 10:23–25 and 1 Thessalonians 5:11, we are reminded that encouragement is not optional, it is essential for the health of the body of Christ. The church grows stronger when its members speak words of life, show up for one another, and build each other up in love. Through encouragement, we help each other hold firmly to our confession of hope, stir one another to love and good works, and prepare our hearts for the coming of the Lord. This lesson reminds us that encouragement doesn't require great skill, only open eyes, willing hearts, and faithful presence. When the people of God become encouragers, the church becomes a place of joy, healing, and unity.

Class Objectives:

By the end of this class, you should be able to:

1. Explain why encouragement is vital to perseverance and unity in the church (Hebrews 10:23–25; 1 Thessalonians 5:11).
2. Describe how gathering together and showing up for others strengthens relationships and faith.
3. Identify simple, practical ways to build others up through words, actions, and prayer.

4. Understand how each act of encouragement strengthens and stabilizes the body of Christ.
5. Reflect on personal or cultural obstacles that prevent encouragement and learn to replace silence with compassion.
6. Make a personal commitment to encourage at least three people this week—by word, by action, and by prayer—as a reflection of Christ's love.

Introduction:

Encouragement has power. It's the spark that reignites weary hearts. It reminds us that our labor matters, that we're seen, valued, and loved. In a world full of criticism, cynicism, and noise, encouragement is the language of grace, and it's one of the most Christlike things we can give to another person.

The Hebrew writer captured this beautifully in Hebrews 10:23–25: *let us hold on to the confession of our hope without wavering, since he who promised is faithful. And let us watch out for one another to provoke love and good works, not neglecting to gather together, as some are in the habit of doing, but encouraging each other, and all the more as you see the Day approaching.* The Christian life is not meant to be lived in isolation. God designed the church to be a community of mutual encouragement, a place where believers hold each other up, stir one another toward love, and strengthen one another's faith. Encouragement isn't just a suggestion; it's a spiritual responsibility.

In 1 Thessalonians 5:11, Paul said: *therefore encourage one another and build each other up as you are already doing.* Every one of us is called to be a builder of faith, to use our words and actions to strengthen those around us.

In today's lesson, we'll see that encouragement strengthens faith, requires presence, and builds the body. It's not complicated or flashy; it's simply love in action. And it's one of the most powerful ways we can reflect the heart of Jesus in the everyday moments of life.

Encouragement Strengthens Faith

The Hebrew writer says, *let us hold on to the confession of our hope without wavering, since He who promised is faithful. And let us watch out for one another to provoke love and good works.* This passage captures two vital truths: faith needs endurance, and endurance needs encouragement. The Christian life is often a long road filled with unexpected valleys. There are days when hope feels dim and obedience feels heavy. That's why God places us in the local church, so that when a brother or sister's faith grows weary, another can speak strength back into it.

1. Encouragement Helps Us Hold On

The command, *let us hold on to the confession of our hope without wavering,* assumes that life will try to shake us. Trials, loss, criticism, and disappointment can all make us feel like letting go. But encouragement acts like a spiritual grip; it reminds us that God's promises are still true and that we are not alone in clinging to them.

When someone looks you in the eye and says, "I believe in what God is doing in you," or "Don't give up, God is faithful," it does something deep inside. It steadies the heart. Encouragement doesn't remove the storm, but it strengthens your anchor in it.

2. Encouragement Is an Act of Spiritual Awareness

Verse 24 says, *let us watch out for one another to provoke love and good works.* The phrase "watch out for" means to pay close attention, to be spiritually alert to the needs of others. It's the opposite of passivity. Encouragement requires attentiveness. You can't build up people you're not looking at.

Encouragement means noticing when someone's faith is flickering and stepping in before it fades. Sometimes it's a note, a prayer, a conversation in the foyer, or a simple "I've been thinking about you." These small acts often have an eternal impact.

In 2010, a group of Chilean miners were trapped underground for 69 days. During the long weeks of waiting for rescue, what kept them alive emotionally was communication, messages from above, reminders that they weren't forgotten. Each note sent down carried hope: "We're still with you. Don't lose heart." That's what encouragement does in the body of Christ. It sends down hope into the dark places of someone's soul and reminds them that they are not forgotten, that God is still working.

3. Encouragement Is a Faith Transfer

When we encourage someone, we're not just offering positive words; we're sharing faith. Our confidence in God becomes contagious. Encouragement says, "I know God's not finished yet, and I'll believe that with you until you see it." That's why encouragement isn't optional; it's essential. Faith was never meant to survive in isolation. It grows in the warmth of fellowship, in the presence of voices that remind us of who God is and what He's promised.

Practically, this means we should look around the church every week and ask: *Who needs to be reminded today that God is still faithful?* When you speak life into another believer, you're helping them hold on to hope, and you're fulfilling the call of Hebrews 10 to strengthen the faith of the family.

Encouragement is not just nice; it's necessary. It's what keeps faith alive in weary hearts.

Encouragement Requires Presence and Intentionality

The Hebrew writer continues: *not neglecting to gather together, as some are in the habit of doing, but encouraging each other, and all the more as you see the Day approaching.* Encouragement doesn't happen by accident; it occurs when believers make a deliberate choice to *show up* for one another. The church is not just a collection of individuals; it's a family. And like any healthy family, encouragement only thrives when its members are present, attentive, and engaged.

1. Encouragement Thrives in Presence

The phrase "not neglecting to gather together" reminds us that physical presence matters. In-person fellowship is God's design for building one another up. You can't fully encourage from a distance. You can text, call, or write, and those are good things, but there's something about seeing someone's face, sharing a meal, or sitting side by side in worship that fills the heart in ways words alone cannot.

The early Christians met regularly, in homes, courtyards, and catacombs, not because it was easy, but because they knew they needed each other. When persecution, fear, or hardship threatened their faith, the gathering of believers renewed their strength.

Encouragement begins with *being there.* Presence is half the ministry.

2. Encouragement Requires Intention

The command to "encourage each other" is active. It means we don't wait until someone looks discouraged, we look for opportunities to build others up before the discouragement even comes. Encouragement is proactive, not reactive.

It might look like noticing someone who's new and making them feel welcome. It might mean calling someone you haven't seen in a while, or writing a note to a young parent, teacher, or servant who's working quietly in the background.

During World War II, the British government launched a morale campaign with three simple posters: "Freedom Is in Peril—Defend It with All Your Might," "Your Courage, Your Cheerfulness, Your Resolution Will Bring Us Victory," and "Keep Calm and Carry On." Those messages became lifelines for a nation under siege. In the same way, spiritual encouragement is how the church keeps morale alive when the world presses in. We remind each other: *God is still good. His promises still stand. You're not alone, keep going.*

3. Encouragement Is Urgent and Ongoing

Notice the urgency in the text: *all the more as you see the Day approaching.* The closer we get to eternity, the more encouragement we need. The pressures of life, the rise of apathy, and the weariness of waiting for Christ's return can make hearts grow cold. That's why encouragement is not a one-time event, it's a continual practice. Encouragement is the fuel of perseverance. It keeps the fire burning in the hearts of God's people as we await the Lord's return.

Practically, this means:

- **Be consistent in gathering.** Don't underestimate the ministry of simply being present.
- **Be intentional in noticing.** Look around you before and after worship. Who seems tired? Who hasn't been there lately?
- **Be generous in speaking life.** A word of hope may be exactly what someone needs to keep pressing on.

The church becomes stronger every time we gather, not just because of sermons or songs, but because of the quiet ministry of believers who show up and encourage one another. Encouragement isn't optional; it's how the church keeps its heart beating.

Encouragement Builds the Body

In 1 Thessalonians 5:11, Paul writes, *therefore encourage one another and build each other up as you are already doing.* This short verse captures one of the most straightforward and powerful truths about church life: encouragement is the building material of the body of Christ. It's how faith grows, how hope stays alive, and how love keeps multiplying. Every word of encouragement you speak adds strength to someone's soul.

1. Encouragement Is Construction Work for the Heart

The phrase, *build each other up,* comes from the language of construction. Just as a builder adds one brick at a time, every believer contributes to the spiritual structure of the church through words and actions of encouragement. The body of Christ doesn't grow stronger by accident; it's built intentionally by believers who speak life and faith into one another. Every kind word, every prayer, every gesture of support is like another stone laid into the wall of someone's faith. Encouragement is the spiritual equivalent of construction work, and every Christian is a builder.

2. Encouragement Strengthens Unity and Stability

Encouragement does more than make people feel good; it makes the church *strong.* A discouraged brother or sister is a vulnerable believer; a discouraged church is a weakened church. But a congregation filled with encouragement becomes a fortress of faith.

Think about the Golden Gate Bridge in San Francisco, one of the most iconic suspension bridges in the world. From a distance, it looks as though two enormous cables hold up the roadway. But each of those cables is made of more than 27,000 individual steel wires, all woven tightly together. No single wire could bear the weight of the bridge alone, but together, they create incredible strength and stability.

That's exactly how encouragement works in the body of Christ. The church doesn't stand firm because of one strong person, but because thousands of small, unseen acts of encouragement are woven together through love. Every kind word, every prayer, every gesture of support adds another strand of strength. And when those strands are bound together in Christ, the church becomes unshakable, able to carry the weight of one another's burdens with grace. Paul says in Ephesians 4:16 that the church "builds itself up in love as each part does its work." Encouragement is every believer's contribution to that ongoing construction project.

3. Encouragement Multiplies Itself

Paul ends the verse by saying, *as you are already doing.* The Thessalonians were already known for their encouragement, and Paul's words push them to keep going. Why? Because encouragement spreads. It's contagious. When you lift someone up, they're more likely to lift someone else.

A church that consistently encourages builds an atmosphere of joy and faith. People walk into that kind of congregation and *feel* the difference, the warmth, the hope, and the genuine care. Encouragement transforms the church from just a place we attend into a family we belong to.

Practically, that means:

- **Be intentional with words.** Compliment spiritual growth, not just performance.
- **Be specific.** "You did a great job leading that prayer" is good; "Your prayer reminded me how faithful God is" is better.
- **Be consistent.** Don't save encouragement for special occasions; make it a daily habit.

Encouragement is not about flattery or false praise; it's about building truth into another person's life. When you encourage, you join God in His building project, shaping hearts, strengthening faith, and holding the body together in love. A church that encourages one another well doesn't just survive; it *thrives.*

Practical Application: How to Encourage One Another

Encouragement is one of the simplest ministries in the church, but it's also one of the most neglected. Too often, we assume people "already know" they're appreciated, valued, or loved. But encouragement only works when it's expressed. The church becomes stronger when its people turn encouragement into a daily discipline.

Here are several practical ways to put this into action:

1. **Speak Life Daily**
   Words have incredible power. Proverbs 18:21 says, *death and life are in the power of the tongue.* Make it a goal every day to speak life into someone else. Tell them how you see God working in them. Say, "I appreciate you," "I believe in you," or "You encouraged me." Don't underestimate how one sentence can lift someone's spirit for an entire week.
2. **Be Present and Attentive**
   Encouragement begins with awareness. You can't build up someone you never notice. Pay attention to who's missing from worship, who looks weary, who's serving quietly without recognition. A text, call, or kind word at the right time can remind them that they're not forgotten.
3. **Write It Down**
   A written note lasts longer than a spoken compliment. Consider writing one encouraging note or message each week. Be specific: mention what you appreciate, how their faith inspires you, or what you've learned from their example. These small acts often become treasures that people hold onto for years.
4. **Celebrate Growth, Not Just Success**
   Encouragement is not about flattery; it's about seeing what God

is doing in someone's life and calling it out. Celebrate faithfulness, repentance, and perseverance, not just accomplishments. A sincere "I see you growing in grace" can mean more than applause for any achievement.

5. **Create an Encouraging Culture**
   Encouragement spreads when it's modeled. If church leaders, Bible class teachers, and members intentionally use words of affirmation, others will follow. Encourage openly in conversations, meetings, and worship. A church filled with encouragement is a church filled with energy, joy, and unity.
6. **Pray for Those You Encourage**
   The greatest encouragement comes through prayer. When you tell someone, "I'm praying for you," and do it, you're carrying their burden to the throne of God. Let them know you've prayed for them; it builds deep trust and spiritual strength.

Challenge

This week, choose three people to encourage intentionally:

1. **By word:** say something uplifting face-to-face.
2. **By action:** do something that helps or blesses them.
3. **By prayer:** intercede for them and follow up.

Keep a simple "Encouragement Journal" for one week. Write down who you encouraged, how they responded, and how it impacted your own spirit. You'll quickly see that encouragement not only builds others, but it also builds *you.*

Conclusion

Encouragement is one of the most Christlike ministries we can practice, because Jesus Himself was the ultimate encourager. He lifted the weary, restored the broken, and strengthened the fainthearted. When others saw failure, He saw potential. When others offered judgment, He offered hope. His words didn't just comfort; they gave life.

That same ministry now belongs to us. The writer of Hebrews calls us to "encourage one another, and all the more as you see the Day approaching." In other words, encouragement isn't optional; it's essential. Every believer has the power to build up someone's faith, to remind them that God is still faithful, and to rekindle the flame of hope in their heart.

We've seen today that encouragement strengthens faith, requires presence, and builds the body. It doesn't take special skill, just a willing heart. A kind word, a note, a prayer, or even a simple smile can lift a soul that's ready to give up. And when encouragement becomes a way of life, it changes the culture of a church. People stop competing and start caring. They stop criticizing and start building.

This week, don't wait for someone else to encourage you; *be* the encourager. Look for those who are tired, discouraged, or unnoticed, and breathe life into them. Speak words that heal instead of harm. Build bridges instead of walls.

Because when we encourage one another, we do more than make people feel good; we make Christ visible. And in a world starved for hope, that may be the most powerful ministry we can offer.

For Discussion

1. Can you think of a time when someone encouraged you at just the right moment? What impact did it have on your faith, attitude, or perseverance?

 ____

 ____

 ____

2. Why do you think encouragement is essential to helping believers "hold on to the confession of our hope without wavering"? How can your words help someone stay anchored in faith?

 ____

 ____

 ____

3. The writer of Hebrews ties encouragement to gathering together. What does that teach us about the importance of showing up, both physically and emotionally, for one another?

___

___

___

4. Paul says encouragement "builds up" the church. What does that mean in practical terms? How can we each become "builders" in our congregation?

___

___

___

5. What sometimes keeps us from encouraging others—fear, busyness, self-focus, or discomfort? How can we overcome those barriers and become more intentional encouragers?

___

___

___

6. Who in your life needs encouragement right now? What specific step will you take this week—a word, note, visit, or prayer—to strengthen that person's faith?

___

___

___

Lesson 12

How to Persevere in Ministry

2 Corinthians 4:7–10; James 1:2–4

Now we have this treasure in clay jars, so that this extraordinary power may be from God and not from us. We are afflicted in every way but not crushed; we are perplexed but not in despair; we are persecuted but not abandoned; we are struck down but not destroyed. We always carry the death of Jesus in our body, so that the life of Jesus may also be displayed in our body, 2 Corinthians 4:7–10.

Consider it a great joy, my brothers and sisters, whenever you experience various trials, because you know that the testing of your faith produces endurance. And let endurance have its full effect, so that you may be mature and complete, lacking nothing, James 1:2–4.

Class Overview: Ministry can be deeply rewarding, but it can also be exhausting. Every servant of God faces moments of discouragement, weakness, and loss. In 2 Corinthians 4:7–10, 16–18 and James 1:2–4, Scripture reminds us that perseverance is not about personal strength but about trusting in God's sustaining power. Paul calls believers "clay jars" carrying a priceless treasure, fragile yet filled with divine strength. Though our outer person grows weary, God renews our inner person daily. James teaches that endurance through trials produces maturity and completeness in Christ. This lesson calls every Christian, preacher, teacher, servant, or encourager, to remain faithful even when ministry feels heavy. When we learn to rely on grace instead of grit, perseverance becomes not a burden but a testimony of God's faithfulness.

Class Objectives:

By the end of this class, you should be able to:

1. Explain how God's power, not human effort, enables endurance in ministry (2 Corinthians 4:7–10)
2. Describe how God renews the "inner person" day by day, even as

physical or emotional strength fades (2 Corinthians 4:16–18).

3. Understand how hardship refines faith and produces spiritual maturity (James 1:2–4).
4. Learn to surrender weakness to God as an act of dependence, not defeat.
5. Identify practices, prayer, rest, fellowship, perspective, that foster perseverance in ministry and life.
6. See endurance not as survival, but as a witness to the faithfulness of God who never gives up on His servants.

Introduction:

1998 WAS A PARTICULARLY TOUGH YEAR IN MY PREACHING CAREER. Trying to do the right thing, I decided to help a state parolee who had been a member of the congregation before I moved there. He appeared to be very spiritual and helped me set up many Bible studies. But he was also very conniving and deceitful as he cheated my wife and me out of thousands of dollars. Previously, I had stood before the congregation affirming my belief in him. Later, it was found out he had outstanding warrants in another state, and he fled to escape being arrested. When this news came out, the critics in the congregation pounced. It was brutal. On top of all the financial and ministry stress, my wife lost our baby. One afternoon, I sat in my office and seriously wondered if it was time to step away. I told God, *"I don't think I can do this anymore."*

After sitting there for a long time in silence, I reached for my Bible. It providentially happened to open to 2 Corinthians 4. My eyes fell on verse 1: *therefore, since we have this ministry because we were shown mercy, we do not give up.* It was like Paul was speaking straight to my heart. I hadn't earned my place in ministry; I'd been given it by grace. And if grace had called me, grace would sustain me.

That moment didn't make all the problems go away, as I spent much of the rest of the year digging out financially and getting back on my feet with my ministry. Still, it did remind me of something I'd forgotten: perseverance isn't about having endless strength, it's about trusting in the endless strength of God.

Every servant of God eventually faces moments like that. Whether you teach, serve, lead, encourage, or quietly help behind the scenes, there will be times when you feel tired, unseen, or discouraged. Paul knew that feeling well. Ministry had cost him dearly, physically, emotionally, and spiritually. Yet he could still write, *we are afflicted in every way but not crushed, perplexed but not in despair, persecuted but not abandoned, struck down but not destroyed* (2 Corinthians 4:8–9).

How could he say that? Because Paul had learned that perseverance is not about avoiding hardship, it's about trusting God during it. He understood that weakness wasn't failure; it was the stage where God's power shines brightest.

James echoed that same truth in his letter when he said, *consider it a great joy… whenever you experience various trials, because you know that the testing of your faith produces endurance* (James 1:2–3). Trials don't destroy real faith, they refine it.

In today's lesson, we'll see that perseverance in ministry grows from three truths:

1. Our strength is limited, but God's power is not.
2. Our outer person may grow weary, but God renews us inwardly every day.
3. Our trials are not wasted: they are shaping us into stronger, wiser servants.

The question isn't *"How can I keep from getting tired?"* but *"Where will I turn when I do?"* If we learn to rely on God's power instead of our own, we'll find that perseverance is not about gritting our teeth, it's about resting in grace.

Perseverance Is Rooted in God's Power

In 2 Corinthians 4, Paul writes, *now we have this treasure in clay jars, so that this extraordinary power may be from God and not from us. We are afflicted in every way but not crushed; we are perplexed but not in despair; we are persecuted but not abandoned; we are struck down but not destroyed. We always carry the death of Jesus in our body, so that the life of Jesus may also be displayed in our body.*

This passage is one of the most honest and encouraging portraits of ministry ever written. Paul doesn't hide the struggle, he embraces it. Ministry, he says, is like being a fragile clay jar carrying a priceless treasure. The jar is weak, but the treasure inside is powerful. The cracks in the vessel don't disqualify us; they become the very means through which God's power shines.

1. Our Weakness Reveals God's Strength

Paul describes himself as afflicted, perplexed, persecuted, and struck down, words that sound like defeat, yet he pairs each one with victory: *not crushed, not in despair, not abandoned, not destroyed.* That's the mystery of perseverance. It's not that we never feel pressure or pain; it's that we endure both without collapsing.

Why? Because the power at work in us doesn't come from us. The same power that raised Jesus from the dead lives in us (Romans 8:11). God allows weakness to remain so that we never mistake the source of our endurance. Our cracks remind the world, and ourselves, that any light shining through us is His, not ours.

In the 16th century, Japanese artists developed a type of pottery repair called *kintsugi,* also known as "golden joinery." When a bowl broke, instead of throwing it away, they repaired it with a lacquer mixed with gold dust. The cracks didn't disappear; they became part of its beauty. The restored vessel was even more valuable than before. That's how God works with us. Our cracks, the scars from struggle and failure, become the places where His grace shines the brightest.

2. Perseverance Flows from Surrender, Not Stubbornness

Sometimes we confuse perseverance with pride, as if pushing harder, working longer, or refusing to rest equals faithfulness. But real perseverance isn't the refusal to fall; it's the willingness to depend. Paul didn't endure because he was tough; he endured because he trusted. His resilience was rooted in reliance. We are not called to be superheroes in ministry. We're called to be servants who lean on supernatural strength. God's power sustains what our human strength cannot.

3. Our Suffering Displays Christ's Life

Paul says, *we always carry the death of Jesus in our body, so that the life of Jesus may also be displayed in our body.* When we persevere through trials, we reflect the gospel itself. The pattern of Jesus' life, death, and resurrection becomes the pattern of our ministry. Every hardship is a reminder that resurrection life comes through suffering, not apart from it.

Every time we keep serving through pain, forgiving after betrayal, or showing up when we feel spent, we are showing the world what resurrection looks like in real life.

Practically, this means:

- When you feel weak, don't hide it. Surrender it to God and let Him work through it.
- When you feel pressure, remember that affliction doesn't mean abandonment.
- When you feel cracked and inadequate, remember that God shines brightest through broken vessels.

Perseverance begins when we stop trying to be strong for God and start trusting that He is strong in us.

Perseverance Renews the Inner Person

In 2 Corinthians 4:16–18, Paul continues his encouragement by saying, *therefore we do not give up. Even though our outer person is being destroyed, our inner person is being renewed day by day. For our momentary light affliction is producing for us an absolutely incomparable eternal weight of glory. So we do not focus on what is seen, but on what is unseen. For what is seen is temporary, but what is unseen is eternal.*

If anyone had reason to quit, it was Paul. He had endured beatings, imprisonment, hunger, betrayal, and exhaustion. Yet his refrain is steady: *we do not give up.* Why? Because he learned to see beyond what was visible. Perseverance depends on perspective.

1. The Outer Person Grows Weary, but the Inner Person Is Renewed

Paul acknowledges reality: ministry is hard. Physically, emotionally, and mentally, it wears us down. He calls this the *outer person,* the part of us that feels fatigue, frustration, and pain. But then he adds something remarkable: while the outer person declines, the *inner person,* the spiritual self, can grow stronger every day.

In other words, you can be worn out physically but still be flourishing spiritually. That's the paradox of perseverance. God uses struggle not to destroy us, but to renew us from the inside out. Every trial that drains your strength becomes an invitation to draw from His.

In 2019, wildfires swept across large portions of Yellowstone National Park. The devastation was shocking; thousands of acres were turned to ash. But within months, something beautiful began to happen. Beneath the burned surface, seeds that could only sprout after fire began to take root. New life covered the landscape. The fire hadn't destroyed the forest; it had awakened it.

That's what God does in our lives. The fires of trial burn away the surface things we depend on, our pride, our control, our comfort, but underneath, He's planting something new. Perseverance allows that new life to grow.

2. Affliction Is Temporary; Glory Is Eternal

Paul calls his hardships "momentary light affliction." That's astounding when you think about everything he endured. But Paul isn't minimizing suffering; he's magnifying eternity. When you weigh your trials against eternity's glory, even the heaviest burdens become light by comparison.

What sustained Paul wasn't the denial of pain but the vision of purpose. He saw that every hardship was *producing an eternal weight of glory.* The word "producing" means working for or accomplishing. Your trials are not meaningless; they're doing something, shaping your soul, deepening your dependence, and preparing you for what's ahead.

3. Perseverance Shifts Our Focus from the Seen to the Unseen

Paul's secret was focus. He refused to live by sight. The things we see, struggles, disappointments, and even successes, are temporary. The things we don't see, God's presence, His promises, and His eternal plan, are what truly last. Faith gives us the lens to look past exhaustion and see redemption. Perseverance doesn't mean ignoring pain; it means seeing purpose beyond it.

Practically, this means:

- **Start each day with renewal, not reaction.** Begin your day in prayer, asking God to refresh your spirit before you face the world.
- **Keep an eternal perspective.** Remind yourself daily: "This is temporary. God is doing something bigger."
- **Feed the inner person.** When life drains you, turn to worship, Scripture, and fellowship. These are the wells that refill the soul.

Paul didn't survive ministry because he was superhuman; he endured because he learned to focus on the unseen and live for what lasts. The more he suffered outwardly, the stronger he became inwardly.

Perseverance Produces Spiritual Maturity

James writes, *consider it a great joy, my brothers and sisters, whenever you experience various trials, because you know that the testing of your faith produces endurance. And let endurance have its full effect, so that you may be mature and complete, lacking nothing,* James 1:2–4. James doesn't say *if* you face trials, he says *whenever.* Trouble is not the exception in ministry; it's the environment in which faith grows. Trials test us, stretch us, and refine us, but their ultimate purpose is transformation. Perseverance isn't just surviving hardship; it's being shaped by it into the likeness of Christ.

1. Trials Are the Training Ground of Faith

James uses the word *testing,* a term from metallurgy. It describes the refining process by which impurities are burned away so that the metal becomes pure and strong. That's what God does through hardship. He tests faith not to destroy it but to develop it. Endurance doesn't grow in comfort; it grows under pressure. Every season of difficulty is a classroom in which God teaches us patience, humility, and trust. Those lessons cannot be learned any other way.

In 1997, the Mars Pathfinder mission sent a small rover named *Sojourner* to explore the surface of Mars. Engineers tested the rover for years in extreme heat, cold, wind, and vibration before launching it. Why? Because they knew it had to survive conditions harsher than anything on Earth. When it landed safely and began sending back data, the testing was vindicated. The same is true for us: God tests His servants on Earth to prepare them for eternal work that will endure forever.

2. Endurance Builds Character, and Character Maturity

James says, *let endurance have its full effect.* In other words, don't quit halfway through the process. God is doing more than getting you through something; He's forming something *in* you. Every challenge you endure faithfully adds another layer of maturity. Romans 5:3–4 teaches the same truth: *we also boast in our afflictions, because we know that affliction produces endurance, endurance produces proven character, and proven character produces hope.* Endurance is the bridge between affliction and hope; it's how we cross from pain to purpose.

3. Perseverance Leads to Spiritual Wholeness

James ends by saying that endurance leads us to be "mature and complete, lacking nothing." Spiritual maturity doesn't come through years of service alone; it comes through faithful perseverance in seasons of struggle. Every difficulty endured with faith makes us more complete, more dependent on grace, and more like Jesus.

This means perseverance is not punishment, it's preparation. God is building spiritual muscle in His people so that we can withstand future challenges and help others do the same.

Practically, this means:

- When trials come, resist the urge to ask, *"Why me?"* Instead, ask, *"What is God teaching me?"*
- Stay faithful in small things. Consistency today becomes endurance tomorrow.
- Remember that maturity is not measured by ease but by faithfulness under pressure.

Every great servant of God, Moses, David, Esther, Paul, and Jesus Himself, learned obedience and strength through suffering. Perseverance is the furnace in which God forges maturity.

So, when you feel stretched, weary, or tested, remember: God is not trying to break you; He's trying to build you.

Practical Application: How to Persevere in Ministry

Perseverance is not about avoiding difficulty; it's about learning to stand firm in the middle of it. Ministry will test your patience, drain your energy, and sometimes leave you wondering whether you're making a difference. But God has given us everything we need to endure faithfully and finish well.

Here are several practical ways to cultivate perseverance in ministry:

1. **Anchor Your Identity in God, Not in Results**
   Discouragement often grows when we measure success by visible outcomes: attendance numbers, reactions, or immediate fruit. Paul reminds us that *"we have this treasure in clay jars"* (2 Corinthians 4:7). The treasure is Christ, not us. Our value isn't in how much we accomplish, but in Who we belong to. When your identity is secure in God, you can keep serving faithfully even when results seem small.
2. **Renew Your Inner Person Daily**
   Paul says our "inner person is being renewed day by day" (2 Corinthians 4:16). Perseverance requires spiritual refueling. Make time for prayer, Scripture, and rest. Ministry without renewal leads to burnout. Guard your quiet time with God as the most important appointment of your day. Renewal doesn't happen by accident; it happens by discipline.
3. **Reframe Trials as Training, Not Punishment**
   James tells us to *consider it great joy* when trials come, because they produce endurance (James 1:2–3). That doesn't mean we enjoy hardship, but that we recognize its purpose. Trials are God's classroom for growth. When challenges arise, ask, "What is God forming in me through this?" instead of "Why is this happening to me?"
4. **Rest Without Quitting**
   Perseverance doesn't mean running yourself into the ground. Even

Jesus withdrew to rest and pray (Mark 1:35). Rest is not weakness; it's wisdom. Know your limits and honor them. Step back when you need to recharge so you can return with strength and clarity.

5. **Surround Yourself with Encouragers**
   Even Paul needed companions like Timothy, Titus, and Barnabas. Isolation breeds despair, but fellowship fuels endurance. Find people who will pray for you, remind you of your calling, and speak life into your weary moments. Perseverance is easier when you're not running alone.
6. **Keep Your Eyes on Eternity**
   Paul endured hardship because he fixed his gaze on what was unseen: the "eternal weight of glory" (2 Corinthians 4:17). Perspective shapes perseverance. When you remember that today's struggles are temporary and eternity is forever, you can keep serving with hope. Ministry is not measured by the moment; it's measured by eternity.

Challenge

This week, take inventory of your heart. Where are you growing weary? Where have you been tempted to give up? Spend time in prayer asking God to renew your inner person. Then take one tangible step of faith, whether it's re-engaging in a ministry task, reconnecting with someone you've drifted from, or simply resting in God's strength- as an act of perseverance.

Conclusion

Perseverance is not about possessing unshakable strength; it's about trusting the God who sustains us when our strength runs out. The Apostle Paul could say, *we do not give up,* not because life was easy, but because grace was sufficient. That same grace still sustains every servant of God today.

Today, what happened to me in 1998 feels like a lifetime ago. I have come through so much since then. New challenges have come and gone. And through them all, God has provided and gotten me through. That knowledge has helped me persevere.

That's what Paul meant when he said, *though our outer person is being destroyed, our inner person is being renewed day by day.* Perseverance doesn't mean we never feel weary; it means we keep walking, trusting that God will renew our spirit one day at a time. It means learning to see hardship not as the end of something, but as the place where God's strength begins.

When you feel like quitting, when your heart is tired, your work feels unseen, or your prayers seem unanswered, remember that your ministry exists because of mercy. Grace started it, grace sustains it, and grace will see it through.

You may feel like a clay jar, cracked and fragile, but that's where God's light shines brightest. And when you look back one day, like I can now, you'll see that every scar became a testimony, every struggle a teacher, and every season of weakness another reminder that *we do not give up, because God never gives up on us.*

For Discussion

1. Have you ever faced a moment in your spiritual life or ministry when you felt like giving up? What helped you endure, and what did you learn about God through that experience?

   ____

   ____

   ____

2. Paul describes himself as a "clay jar" holding a priceless treasure. How does this image help you understand your own weakness and God's strength? What does it mean to let God's power shine through your cracks?

   ____

   ____

   ____

3. What are some ways your "inner person" can be renewed daily, even when your "outer person" feels exhausted or overwhelmed? How can you practically cultivate spiritual renewal in your own life?

___

___

___

4. How have your own trials shaped your faith and character over time? What does it mean to "let endurance have its full effect" in the middle of a difficult season?

___

___

___

5. Paul called his afflictions "momentary and light" because he focused on eternal glory. How does an eternal perspective change the way you see present hardships in ministry or life?

___

___

___

6. Matthew shared a story from 1998 when God used a difficult season to renew his calling. What is one painful or wearying experience in your own life that God might be using to teach perseverance? How can you trust His grace to sustain you right now?

___

___

___

Lesson 13

How to Finish Faithfully

2 Timothy 4:6–8; Revelation 2:10

For I am already being poured out as a drink offering, and the time for my departure is close. I have fought the good fight, I have finished the race, I have kept the faith. There is reserved for me the crown of righteousness, which the Lord, the righteous Judge, will give me on that day, and not only to me, but to all those who have loved his appearing, 2 Timothy 4:6–8.

Don't be afraid of what you are about to suffer. Look, the devil is about to throw some of you into prison to test you, and you will experience affliction for ten days. Be faithful to the point of death, and I will give you the crown of life, Revelation 2:10.

Class Overview: Every Christian begins the race of faith with enthusiasm, but not everyone finishes well. In *2 Timothy 4:6–8* and *Revelation 2:10*, the apostle Paul and the Lord Jesus both call believers to endurance—to remain faithful to the end, no matter the cost. Finishing faithfully is not about perfection or recognition; it's about steady devotion and trust in the grace of God. Paul viewed his life as an offering poured out for the glory of Christ, confident that the same Lord who called him would also reward him. The faithful Christian runs with purpose, keeps their eyes fixed on eternity, and relies on God's strength rather than their own. This final lesson in the *Tools for Ministry* series reminds us that faithfulness is the goal of every servant—to complete the race, keep the faith, and receive the crown of life from the righteous Judge who never forgets His own.

Class Objectives:

By the end of this class, you should be able to:

1. Explain Paul's reflection on his ministry and what it reveals about living with an eternal perspective (2 Timothy 4:6–7).
2. Describe how faithful endurance is essential to finishing well, even when the path is marked by hardship and loss.

3. Understand the meaning of the "crown of righteousness" and "crown of life" as eternal rewards for those who remain faithful (2 Timothy 4:8; Revelation 2:10).
4. Learn to value spiritual integrity and steadfast obedience over outward success or acclaim.
5. Identify daily disciplines and attitudes that cultivate endurance, gratitude, and unwavering faith.
6. Reflect on how God's mercy carries His servants through every trial and gives strength to finish the race with joy.

Introduction:

DURING THE LATE 1980S, I WAS A LONG-DISTANCE RUNNER for my junior high and high school track team. My running "career" actually started in 6th grade in 1986. Our community hosted a festival called "Brickfest." Our town was known as the brick capital of the world because Malvern produced more bricks from its three brick plants than any other place on the planet. Our county is famous for a special clay that, after firing in the kiln, results in bricks with a beautiful, natural white color. So, our community leaders felt that this was something we all needed to celebrate with a festival. Each year, there was a 5K race on Saturday morning. The night before, they held a one mile "kids' run" at one of the local brick plants for children from 7th grade and below. That year, I won the race! And it wasn't even close. From there, I began running almost every day. I couldn't wait until next year to run in the 5K with all the adults.

Finally, the following year arrived. On race day, I started strong. The first few miles felt easy, the crowd cheered me on, and I felt good. But somewhere past the second mile, my legs started to ache, my lungs burned, and my confidence began to fade. I thought about quitting more than once. Then, near the end, as we came back into downtown, I saw the finish line in the distance. Something inside me shifted. I found just enough strength to push through. I finished second in my age group that year. I still have the trophy out in my barn. (It's made of brick, so it hasn't fallen apart after all these years.) Crossing that line didn't make me a great runner, but it taught me a valuable lesson: the joy isn't in how fast you start, it's in how faithfully you finish.

That's exactly the message Paul gives in 2 Timothy 4. By the time he wrote those words, Paul was nearing the end of his life. He was in prison in Rome, awaiting execution. Many of his friends had deserted him. The churches he'd planted were facing challenges. His body was worn down by years of travel, persecution, and hardship. But listen to his tone, it isn't one of despair or defeat. It's one of peace and fulfillment.

He writes, *for I am already being poured out as a drink offering, and the time for my departure is close. I have fought the good fight, I have finished the race, I have kept the faith.* (2 Timothy 4:6–7). Those words represent the heart of a servant who has given everything to Christ and who is ready to meet Him without regret. Paul didn't just live faithfully; he *finished* faithfully. He could look back and say, "I've fought, I've finished, I've kept."

That's what we all want, to come to the end of our lives and ministries and be able to say the same. Not that we were perfect, but that we were faithful. Not that we avoided hardship, but that we trusted God through it. Not that we accomplished everything, but that we gave ourselves fully to the One who called us.

In Revelation 2:10, Jesus told the church in Smyrna, *be faithful unto death, and I will give you the crown of life.* That's the goal; it's not just to start strong but to remain faithful all the way to the end.

As we conclude this quarter's study, we'll consider what it means to finish well: to keep the proper perspective, persevere through challenges, and focus on the eternal reward. Because ultimately, the race isn't about who finishes first; it's about who remains faithful.

Finishing Faithfully Requires Perspective

In 2 Timothy 4:6–7, Paul writes, *for I am already being poured out as a drink offering, and the time for my departure is close. I have fought the good fight, I have finished the race, I have kept the faith.* These are the words of a man who saw his life through the lens of eternity. Paul's circumstances were grim, chained in a Roman prison, awaiting execution, yet he spoke with peace and confidence. The key to his endurance was perspective. He viewed his life not as something to cling to, but as something to pour out for God's glory.

1. Faithful Servants See Life as an Offering, not a Possession

When Paul says, *I am being poured out as a drink offering,* he uses a vivid image from Old Testament worship. A drink offering was wine poured out before the Lord at the base of the altar, completely given, with nothing held back. It was an act of total devotion. Paul viewed his ministry that way, not as something to protect or preserve, but as something to give. Every sermon preached, every mile traveled, every scar earned was part of his offering to God. He didn't see his life as his own; it belonged entirely to the One who saved him.

Perspective changes everything. When we see life as an offering instead of a possession, service becomes joy, not duty. Suffering becomes meaningful, not wasted. And finishing well becomes less about preserving comfort and more about pouring out love. In ancient Greece, runners in the Olympic Games didn't compete for money or fame; they ran for the honor of their city and the approval of their king. At the finish line stood a judge holding a crown of olive leaves, waiting to reward the faithful runner who finished the race. The goal wasn't simply to start strong or to outpace others, it was to finish with integrity, representing one's city well. Paul understood that image. He ran not for personal glory, but to honor his King.

2. Faithful Servants Accept the Reality of Departure

Paul says, *the time for my departure is close.* The word "departure" (*analusis*) means "to loosen" or "to untie." It was used to describe a ship being untied from its moorings and setting sail for home. For Paul, death wasn't an end; it was a release. He was about to leave the prison of mortality and sail toward the presence of Christ. That's the perspective of faith: to view death not as defeat, but as departure, not as loss, but as gain. When we live with eternity in view, we no longer fear the end. We see it as the moment when faith becomes sight.

3. Faithful Servants Keep Their Eyes on the Eternal Goal

Paul's perspective shaped his purpose. He could say, *I have fought the good fight.* The "good fight" wasn't a battle against people but against sin, discouragement, and the forces of darkness. He had fought to remain faithful to the gospel in a hostile world. Faithfulness requires focus. If we lose sight of eternity, the struggles of ministry will feel overwhelming. But when we remember that every sermon, every act of service, every unseen labor has eternal weight, we gain strength to keep going.

Practically, this means:

- View every act of service as part of your offering to God.
- Remember that faithfulness matters more than recognition.
- Keep your eyes fixed on eternity: the finish line where your King waits.

Paul could face death without regret because he had already given his life away. That's the perspective that allows us to finish faithfully. When life is seen as an offering, the end is not loss, it's fulfillment.

Finishing Faithfully Requires Perseverance

Paul declares, *I have finished the race.* It's a simple phrase, but it carries enormous weight. Finishing well requires endurance. Anyone can start a race, but far fewer cross the finish line. Paul's words remind us that the Christian life, and ministry especially, is not a sprint but a marathon. It's a long obedience in the same direction, requiring courage, discipline, and faith when the road grows difficult.

1. Perseverance Means Staying the Course When It Would Be Easier to Quit

Suffering, beatings, imprisonment, betrayal, and hardship marked Paul's journey. Yet he could still say, *I have finished the race.* Why? Because his commitment to Christ outweighed his desire for comfort. Every servant of God will face seasons when quitting seems easier than continuing. The temptation to walk away, to withdraw, or to stop caring can be powerful. But perseverance says, *I will keep going, not because it's easy, but because God is worthy.*

During the 1968 Olympics in Mexico City, Tanzanian runner John Stephen Akhwari entered the marathon with high hopes. But early in the race, he fell, dislocating his knee and injuring his shoulder. Most assumed he would quit. Hours after the winner crossed the finish line, Akhwari limped into the stadium, bloodied and exhausted. When asked why he hadn't stopped, he said, *My country didn't send me 5,000 miles to start the race; they sent me to finish it.* That's the spirit God calls us to. The goal is not speed but faithfulness. God didn't call us to start the race; He called us to finish it.

2. Hope, Not Pride fuels Perseverance

Paul's strength didn't come from personal pride or stubborn willpower. It came from confidence in God's promises. He knew that the same Lord who called him would carry him to the end.

Hebrews 12:1–2 gives the same picture: *let us run with endurance the race that lies before us, keeping our eyes on Jesus, the pioneer and perfecter of our faith.* The secret to endurance is focus, not on the pain of the present but on the purpose of the race. When you keep your eyes on Jesus, the finish line becomes worth every step.

3. Perseverance Requires Faithful Consistency, Not Flashy Moments

Finishing faithfully doesn't mean doing something spectacular at the end; it means living consistently along the way. Paul didn't end well because of one heroic moment; he finished well because of thousands of small, unseen acts of obedience. In ministry, it's often the daily faithfulness, the quiet prayers, the late-night visits, the steady teaching, the unseen service, that God uses most powerfully.

Practically, this means:

- **Stay focused** when ministry feels monotonous. God values faithfulness over excitement.
- **Keep showing up.** Perseverance is built on consistency, not convenience.
- **Trust the process.** Growth and fruit come in God's timing, not ours.

Paul's words echo through the centuries: *I have finished the race.* He didn't finish because he was strong; he finished because he refused to stop. Perseverance isn't about perfection; it's about endurance rooted in faith.

Finishing Faithfully Receives a Promise

Paul concludes his reflection on life and ministry with these triumphant words: *there is reserved for me the crown of righteousness, which the Lord, the righteous Judge, will give me on that day, and not only to me, but to all those who have loved his appearing,* 2 Timothy 4:8. And to the church in Smyrna, Jesus says in Revelation 2:10, *be faithful to the point of death, and I will give you the crown of life.* These verses remind us that faithfulness is not forgotten. The race may be long, the battle may be hard, but there is a reward waiting for every servant who endures, not the applause of men, but the approval of God.

1. The Crown Is a Symbol of Victory and Vindication

In Paul's day, victors in athletic contests were awarded a wreath, a crown made of olive or laurel leaves. It wasn't made of gold or jewels, but it symbolized honor, recognition, and achievement. Paul uses that image to describe the reward God will give to those who remain faithful. This "crown of righteousness" isn't something we earn through our own goodness; it's the reward of grace given to those who have trusted and obeyed Christ. It represents final vindication, the moment when God declares, *You have run well. You are mine.*

When a soldier completes his final deployment and returns home, there's often a ceremony: flags, medals, words of honor. But what matters most to that soldier isn't the medal; it's hearing the commanding officer say, *Well done. You served with honor.* That's the moment of validation. That's the image Paul paints here, standing before the Lord, hearing the righteous Judge say, *Well done, good and faithful servant.*

2. The Crown Is Given by the Righteous Judge

Notice who gives the crown: *the Lord, the righteous Judge.* Earthly judges had condemned Paul unjustly, but the true Judge would set things right. The same hands that once bore nails will one day place the crown of life on the heads of those who endured. That's what makes the promise so personal, it's not about getting a trophy; it's about receiving it from the Savior Himself. To see His face, to hear His voice, to know it was all worth it, that's the reward.

3. The Crown Is Promised to All Who Love His Appearing

Paul makes it clear that this promise isn't just for apostles or preachers, it's for *all those who have loved His appearing.* Faithful endurance is within reach for every believer. If you love Jesus, if you long for His return, if you keep walking by faith even when life is hard, this promise is for you. We find similar assurance in Revelation 2:10: *be faithful unto death, and I will give you the crown of life.* The finish line of faith is not death; it's life eternal. For the faithful, death is not defeat; it's the doorway to reward.

Practically, this means:

- Keep eternity in view: every act of faithfulness brings you one step closer to seeing Christ.
- Remember that God keeps perfect records: no tear, sacrifice, or act of service goes unnoticed.
- Encourage one another with the promise of the crown: remind weary believers that glory awaits.

When Paul spoke of his coming crown, he wasn't boasting; he was testifying. The God who called him had kept him. The faith he had fought for would soon be fulfilled. And the same promise stands for us: *If we remain faithful to the end, we will see His face, we will hear His "Well done," and we will wear the crown of life.*

Practical Application: How to Finish Faithfully

Finishing faithfully isn't something that happens by accident. It's the result of daily choices, humble dependence on God, and a heart that longs more for eternity than for earthly applause. Paul didn't finish strong because his path was easy. He finished because he lived with purpose, perseverance, and perspective.

Here are several practical ways to cultivate that same faithfulness:

1. **Live Each Day with Eternity in Mind**
   Paul viewed his life through the lens of eternity. He saw death not as an ending, but as a departure: a transition to what truly matters. The finish line shaped every step of his journey. Ask yourself daily: *What will matter 100 years from now?* When eternity becomes your

focus, priorities shift. Bitterness fades, fear lessens, and faithfulness becomes your goal.

2. **Keep Your Heart Anchored in Grace, Not Performance**
   Paul could say, *I have kept the faith,* not because he was flawless, but because he trusted in God's mercy. Finishing well doesn't mean never falling; it means never letting failure have the last word. Keep coming back to grace. Let it fuel your service, heal your wounds, and keep your heart humble.
3. **Stay Consistent in the Small Things**
   Faithfulness isn't built in grand moments; it's built in quiet consistency. Keep teaching, serving, praying, and showing up even when no one notices. Paul didn't measure his ministry by public success but by private devotion. Finish your assignments with the same diligence you started them.
4. **Pass the Baton to Others**
   In the same letter, Paul told Timothy, *what you have heard from me… commit to faithful men who will be able to teach others also* (2 Timothy 2:2). Finishing well means investing in others who will continue the race after you. Mentoring, training, and encouraging the next generation is part of how we "finish" faithfully.
5. **Guard Your Integrity Until the End**
   Faithfulness is not just about staying active; it's about staying true. Many begin well but falter morally or spiritually along the way. Protect your heart. Keep short accounts with God. Stay transparent, humble, and accountable. The most incredible legacy you can leave is not your accomplishments but your character.
6. **Anticipate the Joy of Hearing, "Well Done"**
   The promise of the "crown of righteousness" (2 Timothy 4:8) is meant to motivate us. Picture that moment: standing before the Lord, seeing His face, hearing Him say, *you were faithful.* That vision has carried countless servants through hardship. Let it carry *you.*

Challenge

This week, take time to reflect on your spiritual race. Where are you strong? Where are you weary? Where do you need to realign your focus?

Write a few short sentences describing the kind of Christian, servant, and finisher you want to be. Pray over it daily. Then live this week in light of that goal, because every small act of faith today prepares you for a faithful finish tomorrow.

Conclusion

Finishing faithfully is not about perfection; it's about endurance. It's about walking with Christ long enough, and closely enough, that His strength carries you when your own runs out. Paul's final words in 2 Timothy 4 are not the sigh of a tired man: they're the song of a fulfilled servant. After decades of hardship, persecution, and sacrifice, he could say with confidence, *I have fought the good fight, I have finished the race, I have kept the faith.* That's the goal for every one of us. To reach the end of our days not bitter or burned out, but grateful, able to say, "I've poured out my life for Christ, and it was worth it."

There will be times along the way when faith feels heavy and ministry feels lonely. There will be losses, disappointments, and seasons when your efforts seem unseen. But as Paul reminds us, *"The Lord, the righteous Judge,"* sees it all, and He has reserved a crown for every faithful servant. One day, every tear, every prayer, every act of obedience will be remembered and rewarded. The finish line is closer than we think. And when we cross it, we will not regret the miles we've run for the glory of God.

When I think back to the struggles I've faced in ministry: the failures, the betrayals, the weary seasons where I wasn't sure I could keep going, I'm reminded of one truth: God has never failed me. The same grace that called me has carried me. The same mercy that sustained me in 1998 still sustains me today. Through every new challenge, God has provided and gotten me through. That knowledge has helped me persevere.

And now, as I look ahead, I want to finish the way Paul did, faithful, thankful, and full of hope. Because the race is not about outpacing others; it's about keeping your eyes on Jesus until you see Him face to face. So, here's the challenge: run your race well. Don't stop short. Don't let bitterness, fear, or fatigue steal your faith. Keep your eyes fixed on the eternal crown, the joy of hearing your Savior say, *well done, good and faithful servant.* Finish faithfully: not for applause, but for the glory of the One who ran before you, endured the cross, and now waits at the finish line with open arms.

For Discussion

1. When you think about your life and ministry, what does "finishing faithfully" look like to you? Who in your life has modeled that kind of endurance and integrity?

   ____

   ____

   ____

2. Paul viewed his life as a "drink offering," poured out for God. How does this image challenge our tendency to cling to comfort, recognition, or control? What would it look like to live with that same perspective of total surrender?

   ____

   ____

   ____

3. Why do you think so many people begin well but fail to finish well? What daily habits or spiritual disciplines help you stay consistent when ministry or faith feels hard?

   ____

   ____

   ____

4. Paul and John both spoke of a "crown of righteousness" and a "crown of life." How does this promise of eternal reward strengthen you to stay faithful now?

   ____

   ____

   ____

5. What does finishing faithfully look like in your current season of life? What steps can you take this week to ensure your focus stays on faithfulness rather than success or recognition?

____

____

____

6. Reflect on Matthew's story about God's sustaining grace through hardship and ministry trials. How have you seen God's faithfulness carry you through difficult seasons? How can that memory fuel your perseverance as you continue your race?

____

____

____

Epilogue: The Work Goes On

Ministry is not a program to complete or a checklist to master; it's a life to live. It's the quiet, daily decision to serve God faithfully where He has placed you, with whatever strength He provides. Over the past thirteen weeks, we've explored how to read and apply Scripture, how to pray with purpose, how to forgive, encourage, and persevere. We've looked deeply into what it means to serve with compassion, handle conflict biblically, and finish faithfully. But in the end, these lessons aren't just about learning how to *do* ministry. They're about learning how to *be* ministers: people whose hearts reflect the heart of Christ.

The longer you serve, the more you'll realize that ministry is not about control or perfection; it's about trust. God doesn't call us because we're capable. He calls us because He's faithful. The clay jar is fragile, but the treasure inside: His Spirit, His Word, His power, is unbreakable.

There will always be seasons when you question whether you're making a difference. Sometimes the results will seem small, the fruit invisible, the labor heavy. But remember Paul's words: *we do not give up. Even though our outer person is being destroyed, our inner person is being renewed day by day* (2 Corinthians 4:16). The reward for faithful service is not recognition in this life, but renewal for the life to come.

When I look back on the journey that led to this study, the triumphs, the setbacks, the prayers prayed in tears, I can say with certainty that God has never once failed me. His grace has been enough. The same God who carried me through heartbreak and exhaustion has carried me through every year since. And I've learned that perseverance isn't about holding on tighter, it's about letting God hold you closer.

As you close this book, remember: your ministry isn't ending here; it's beginning again. Every conversation, every act of kindness, every prayer whispered on behalf of someone else is another opportunity to build up the body of Christ. Keep reading the Word. Keep praying. Keep forgiving. Keep encouraging. Keep running.

And when the road grows long, remember the finish line. Picture the Savior waiting there: arms open, eyes full of joy, crown in hand. Hear His words echo through eternity: *Well done, good and faithful servant. Enter into the joy of your Lord.*

Until that day, may you keep pressing forward: steady, grateful, and faithful, trusting that your labor in the Lord is never in vain.

Matthew Allen

Matthew

October 2025

www.ingramcontent.com/pod-product-compliance
Lightning Source LLC
LaVergne TN
LVHW010320070426
835513LV00025B/2433